The Formula Book

The Formula Book

NORMAN STARK

SHEED AND WARD, INC.

Subsidiary of Universal Press Syndicate

KANSAS CITY

CAUTION TO READERS

In writing *The Formula Book,* I have excluded hazardous materials wherever possible, but in some cases they must be included to make a product effective. In making a formula, the reader should observe any note of caution added at the end of the recipe and consult Appendix F (Definitions of Chemicals) for cautions which may be specific to any ingredient.

We all know that materials such as waxes and oils will burn, so I have concentrated the warnings to materials that may be less familiar. But remember, *all* chemicals, including ordinary table salt, should be kept out of the reach of children, carefully labeled, and used only for the purpose they are intended.

The value and safety to you of the products in this book depends upon your careful use of the materials shown in the proportions given, as well as your observing any special cautions appearing in the book or with the materials. Neither I nor the publisher can be responsible for the efficacy of the products or your own safety if you do not follow these instructions and precautions.

THE FORMULA BOOK © 1975 by Stark Research Corporation. All rights reserved. Printed in the United States of America. No part of this book may be used or reproduced in any manner whatsoever without written permission except in the case of brief quotations embedded in critical articles and reviews. For information address Sheed and Ward, Inc., a subsidiary of Universal Press Syndicate, 6700 Squibb Road, Mission, Kansas 66202.

Library of Congress Card Catalog Number: 75-17054

ISBN: 0-8362-0629-0 (cloth)
ISBN: 0-8362-0630-4 (paper)

Contents

FOREWORD   vii

INTRODUCTION: Why; Basic Equipment; Raw Materials
and Where to Get Them; Some Helpful Hints   ix

1. AROUND THE HOUSE   17
   Floor Care   17
   Furniture Care and Some Other Treatments for Wood   24
   Dishwashing Help   28
   Laundry Help   31
   Shoes and Leather   34
   General Cleaning and Polishing   35
   Fires in Their Places and Out of Them   42
   Controlling Bugs and Other Pests   47
   Paints and Brushes   50
   In the Kitchen   52
   Miscellaneous Home Goodies   56

2. PERSONAL   62
   Making Soap   62
   Hair Care   64
   Body Things   68
   Hands and Face   73
   Teeth   79
   Eyes   80
   Feet   81

3. AUTOMOTIVE AND MECHANICAL   83
   Taking Care of the Outside   84
   Taking Care of the Inside   86
   Cleaning Up   90

4. GARDEN, AGRICULTURAL, AND LIVESTOCK   92

     Caring for Your Plants and Garden   93

     Getting Rid of Pests   97

     For the Animals   100

5. FOR SPORTS AND CAMPING   102

6. SAFETY AND FIRST AID   108

APPENDICES

     Appendix A: Formula Ingredients and Their Metric Equivalents   112

     Appendix B: The Four Categories of Formulas Found in *The Formula Book*   153

     Appendix C: Conversion Equivalents   155

     Appendix D: Temperature Conversion Tables   160

     Appendix E: Sources of Chemicals   161

     Appendix F: Definitions of Chemicals Used in *The Formula Book*   168

     Appendix G: A Treatise on Denatured Alcohols   184

     Appendix H: Selection of Materials   193

     Appendix I: Utensils and Equipment   195

     Appendix J: Illustrations   197

     Appendix K: Formulating Procedures   200

INDEX   205

Foreword

The book you are holding has been developed from an internationally popular supplementary textbook known as *The Formula Manual*. Its current widespread use both here and abroad in schools and colleges, community colleges, adult education and "consumer chemistry" courses has led me to produce a version for the general reader that would be useful in the home workshop or, indeed, the average kitchen. I have simplified it somewhat, leaving out technical details wherever possible, omitting the extended discussions of various scientific principles that are useful in the classroom but might bore the person who is interested in results more than theory, and adapting the "formulas" into "recipe" form, so that they might easily be concocted by anyone who knows how to hard boil an egg.

I would like to express here my thanks to Dr. Ed Nigh of the University of Arizona for his invaluable technical assistance, to my many friends who gave me the encouragement and motivation to write this version of the book, and to the literally thousands of teachers and students, users of the classroom edition, who have volunteered their thoughts, suggestions, and criticisms of which I have made free use in my attempts to improve the work and make it more useful.

Foreword

Introduction

WHY

This book is intended for a variety of people: the handyman, or woman, who enjoys doing a bit of home maintenance, gardening, or minor auto repairs and tune-ups; the family who has suddenly found that inflation has eaten up its vacation budget and is looking around for some new and interesting things to do that don't require traveling hundreds of miles to get to, and that will help save a little cash for when they *can* get around to a traveling vacation; the country dweller who is trying to be more self-sufficient and learn something about how things work; and the many just plain curious people who aren't particularly excited about getting their hands covered with black grease, their clothes spattered with paint, or their backs tired with hoeing a garden, but who might enjoy a relatively clean, easy, and interesting hobby, which will actually be useful and save them money.

For those of you who flunked high-school chemistry and feel a bit uncomfortable at the thought of playing the sorcerer's apprentice, fear not. If you've ever made pancakes from the recipe off the box you can follow all the instructions in this book with good results. In fact, you might think of this as a recipe book, only you don't eat the results. You use them to kill roaches, keep away mosquitoes, clean your hands, polish your floors, mothproof your clothes, preserve leather, and lots more.

Of course, just as you can buy a finely prepared meal in a restaurant—well, some restaurants at any rate—you can also buy a ready-made cucumber skin lotion or glass cleaner, for example. But consider what you're paying for besides the ingredients. There's that pretty little can or bottle that it comes in, the packaging that some well-paid designer dreamed up just to catch your eye; there's the cost of distributing it to the retail stores across the country; an advertising budget that would considerably reduce the national debt; and finally the manufacturer's profit and the retailer's profit. Begin to get the idea?

The reason most of us don't eat all our meals in restaurants is that it's cheaper, more fun, and often more satisfying to eat at home. Likewise, I hope that in using this book you experience at least a part of the fun and satisfaction I have had in compiling and testing it.

Many of the recipes are for fairly modern products such as dishwashing detergent, but there are also a few that are simple old-fashioned ways of doing things that really work. Many old-fashioned methods tend to get forgotten, what with all the fancy stuff for doing the same things on the supermarket shelves. But if the old way works as well or better, and is less expensive, it seems a shame to replace it by something that's more expensive and usually doesn't work any better.

BASIC EQUIPMENT

Most of what you will need is probably around the kitchen already, but it's nice to know more or less what you will need before you get started. You may want to duplicate some of your kitchen utensils for this special purpose, and of course you can improvise. This is a suggested list only. It is handy to have two Pyrex double boilers; several recipes require heating two separate ingredients in this way, and the glass pots have two advantages. You can see what's going on inside, and they are easy to clean. In addition, a set of large mixing bowls, two or three measuring cups, a standard set of kitchen measuring spoons, and a couple of wooden spoons for mixing and stirring are useful. A plastic cone and filter paper such as that sold for making coffee, can be used to filter small undissolved particles out of a liquid to make it clearer and prettier, and of course you will need some containers for your finished products. Jars, bottles, and cans, all with lids, and plastic squeeze bottles, or anything else you can think of can be used. Be sure to label all containers, both those holding finished products and those containing raw materials and keep them well out of the reach of children. A more detailed description of utensils and equipment useful for making formulas in *The Formula Book* is found in Appendix I. Appendix J contains illustrations of many of these utensils.

RAW MATERIALS AND WHERE TO GET THEM

Chemicals aren't always just chemicals. Some are fairly pure, while others have bits of dust, lint, water, and other foreign matter in them. The pure grades are designated as U.S.P. and the less pure ones are designated either Manufacturing or Technical grade. U.S.P. stands for United States Pharmacopoeia, which means they meet government standards set forth in the U.S.P. book for required purity in chemicals for pharmacological use, that is, they are acceptable for both patent and prescription medicines. Manufacturing or Technical grades have lower standards of purity and are, of course, considerably lower in cost, so they should be used wherever possible. However, if you're using magnesium sulfate (Epsom salts) in something to take internally, for example, you need the U.S.P. grade. If you are making something to use as a foot bath or to spray on your plants, then the Technical grade would do as well, depending on how you feel about your feet or your begonias. An extended discussion on the selection of materials is found in Appendix H.

On the subject of alcohol a great deal could be said. There are many different kinds of alcohol that can be made in many different ways for many different purposes. Perhaps the most important fact to remember is that the most common alcohol, called variously ethyl alcohol, ethanol, or grain alcohol, is the only one that can be taken orally, and then only in moderate quantities and diluted by at least an equal amount of water or some other liquid. If you put an "m" in front of it, you get methyl alcohol, called also methanol, or wood alcohol, a violent poison which causes convulsions, blindness, and death. Two other common alcohols, butyl and isopropyl, are moderately poisonous.

Where ethyl alcohol is available for use in beverages for human consumption, it is highly taxed by federal and state governments. Where it is not sold for use in beverages, it is not taxed, and so is much less expensive. But to make sure the alcoholic beverage tax is not evaded, the law requires that ethyl alcohol for nonbeverage uses be adulterated by the addition of some substance which makes it unfit to drink. This adulterated ethyl alcohol is called denatured alcohol. Some of the most common denaturants are benzene, gasoline, kerosene, and methyl alcohol. There are quite a few different types of denatured alcohol for different purposes, but for ours, wherever denatured alcohol is called for as an ingredient, if a specific type is recommended for that use the number will be included. The types of alcohol and their various uses are described more fully in Appendix G.

In almost all cases isopropyl alcohol can be used as a substitute for denatured alcohol. Generally it is less toxic and lower in cost. Your choice should be based on the availability and cost of the two types. Isopropyl alcohol does have a pleasant odor which dissipates as it evaporates. However, in applications such as cologne, this scent may be at odds with the perfume in the product. So, for an application such as this, denatured alcohol would be preferable.

In some applications alcohol is specified to be taken internally, such as in extracts, etc. Here, neither denatured or isopropyl alcohol can be used. Ethyl alcohol is the only alternative. In many areas this can be purchased from a local liquor store under the name ethyl alcohol, but in other areas you may have to settle for vodka, which is about the same.

The most convenient place to buy your raw materials is at the drugstore. There are several large drug companies with well-known brand names, so pick one in your area, go to the retail outlet, and ask the druggist. If he doesn't have what you need, he can usually either order it for you or tell you where to get it. Walgreen, Rexall, and McKesson are three of the largest and best known drug companies that sell chemicals in small quantities, and if none of them has a retail outlet in your town you may be able to order direct from one of their main offices by getting the address from the label of one of their products. Another excellent company that has sold scientific equipment to schools and colleges for years, and also sells hundreds of different chemicals in small quantities, is Ward's Natural Science Establishment, Inc. You can get their catalogue by writing to them at either Box 1712, Rochester, N.Y. 14603, or Box 1749, Monterey, Cal. 93940. There are also chemical supply companies in most cities, you can check the Yellow Pages of the telephone directory and make a few phone calls to locate what you need. In addition, some petroleum products are best obtained from an oil dealer. Ask at your local service station, or call the office of the oil distributor nearest you.

For the convenience of the reader, a listing of all the chemicals used in *The Formula Book* and their usual sources of supply will be found in Appendix E. Following the sources of supply is the number of times that particular chemical is called for in *The Formula Book*. This should give the reader some idea, when he finds it necessary to purchase a chemical in a larger quantity than that called for in a particular formula, to know how many other uses he can put it to. Appendix E also lists some mail-order sources of chemicals, if they cannot be found locally.

SOME HELPFUL HINTS

You may be thinking, "If the smallest amount I can buy is one pound but I only need one ounce, what am I going to do with the rest?" For those of you who think that this might be a problem, we have a couple of suggestions. Nearly all chemicals will keep indefinitely if they are stored in good containers and are protected from moisture, so your one-pound supply can last you two years or twenty, depending on how much is used at a time. With inflation, there is a certain amount of security in knowing that you have, say, a five- or ten-year supply of something. Another excellent idea is to enter into some form of cooperative arrangement with your friends or neighbors. An increasing number of marketing cooperatives are forming across the country, allowing people to buy groceries at wholesale prices and share them among the members of the cooperative. Exactly the same sort of thing could easily be done whenever buying in bulk is necessary. I hasten to add that not all of the products in this book need be bought in bulk. Many of the raw materials you will be using can be bought in small enough quantities to make it reasonable for an individual to produce these things for himself, even on a short-term basis.

A friend of mine once said, with respect to cooking, that whenever she tries a new recipe, she reads it through carefully three times before starting. I have found this to be excellent advice. Don't try to memorize the procedure, but do become familiar with it before you begin.

Although high precision is not required, measurements should be reasonably accurate. Teaspoons and tablespoons are level spoonfuls unless it is otherwise noted. The same is true for cups, half cups, and so on.

A "speck" is a measure that is not often used, but it is defined as the amount of material that will lie within a 1/4 inch square marked on a piece of paper or a note card.

If you need to measure, say, 1/3 cup of some lumpy solid material such as paraffin that can't be easily packed into a measuring cup, you might use this method: Fill the cup to the 2/3 cup line with water, then drop in lumps of the material until the water reaches the 1 cup line. The amount of material you have put in will be 1/3 cup. Of course you cannot use this method with a material that is water soluble or that would be difficult to dry.

Eventually we will all have to make an adjustment to the metric system. Therefore, for the convenience of the reader, the ingredients in the recipes are repeated in Appendix A along with their metric equivalents. A detailed explanation of conversion equivalents can be found in Appendix C. Likewise, to give this book an "international" application, Appendix D gives a conversion table of Fahrenheit to centigrade temperatures.

Many things that are beneficial can also be dangerous when improperly used. Electricity, wired in conformance with a code, is a safe dependable energy source. But improperly used, it can become a destructive force. Gas is also an important energy source that is safe when properly used. When it is not, it becomes a potentially lethal force. The automobile is a necessary means of transportation which is safe when properly operated, but uncontrolled can be an instrument of death.

Chemicals are no exceptions. Properly used for the purpose they are intended, they contribute a great deal to our life style. But improperly used, they can become a threat to safety. Let's take sodium chloride, ordinary table salt, as an example. Most of us use salt daily in our food, and regard it as a safe chemical. But if a child were to consume large quantities of it, serious consequences could be the result.

In writing *The Formula Book*, I have excluded hazardous materials wherever possible, but in some cases they must be included to make a product effective. In making a formula, the reader should observe any note of caution added at the end of the recipe and consult Appendix F (Definitions of Chemicals) for cautions which may be specific to any ingredient.

We all know that materials such as waxes and oils will burn, so I have concentrated the warnings to materials that may be less familiar. But remember, *all* chemicals, including ordinary table salt, should be kept out of the reach of children, carefully labeled, and used only for the purpose they are intended.

And now have fun.

$$\underset{\underset{H}{\overset{H}{|}}}{H-C}-\mathbf{1}-\underset{\underset{H}{\overset{H}{|}}}{C-H}$$

Around the House

FLOOR CARE

For those of us who live in houses, keeping the floor reasonably clean is one of the primary housekeeping tasks with which we are faced. The Japanese solve the problem by taking their shoes off at the door, but we are less civilized and track in all manner of dirt and gravel which muddy up the carpets, scratch the finish of floors, and wear down the tiles, boards, or whatever the floor is made of. After a while the place gets pretty messy if we don't keep after it. Years ago, a friend of mine moved into a third-floor walkup in an old New York brownstone, with a wood floor that had forgotten the last time it had seen a finish. Even after a good scrubbing, it presented a very irregular, mottled, brownish-gray appearance. One way of dealing with such a floor, without covering up the wood with paint, is to bleach it. This will remove the stains and ground-in dirt and lighten up the poor mistreated wood to something like its original color.

1. Wood Floor Bleach

It is a good idea to remove all the furniture and give the floor a good soap and water scrubbing to remove loose dirt. Now mix 9 parts of sodium metasilicate with 1 part sodium perborate; if you use 18 cups of the first and 2 cups of the second you will have about a pound. Both of these are available at retail drugstores, and both are white crystalline powders soluble in water.

Dissolve a pound of this mixture in a gallon of very hot water, spread it liberally on the floor with a mop, and let it stand for thirty minutes. Thoroughly rinse out your mop and then rinse the floor well with clear water. You may want to re-do spots that are badly stained.

2. Wood Floor Cleaner

If the floor is not in need of such drastic treatment as bleaching, but just needs a good cleaning, here is a preparation that will clean off a lot of grime and at the same time give the wood back some oil that will help preserve it.

Mix together 2 1/4 cups mineral oil and 3/4 cup oleic acid. Both are available in drugstores, or in larger, more economical quantities from an oil dealer or service station. The first is a clear oil which is distilled from petroleum, the second is yellow to red, derived from animal and vegetable oils. Then into that mix 2 tablespoons household ammonia and 5 tablespoons turpentine. Use one cup of this mixture in two quarts of water, applying with a cloth or sponge mop. This does not need to be rinsed unless the floor was quite dirty and remains streaked. (Note: Household ammonia and turpentine are toxic if taken internally and turpentine is flammable.)

3. Wood Floor Liquid Wax

Here are two liquid floor polishes; the first is quite simple, the second contains more wax and gives a harder finish for a floor that gets more traffic. All ingredients but one can be found in most hardware or paint stores. The ceresin wax for the second polish can be obtained from drugstores, ceramics supply stores, or industrial chemical suppliers. Check the Yellow Pages of the telephone book. A few phone calls should locate a source in your area.

For the first one, take 1/8 cup of paraffin, that common white wax that seals the tops of home-made jelly jars, and melt it in the top of a double boiler. Stir it into 1 quart of mineral oil. Allow to cool and transfer to bottles. Apply with a cloth, let dry, and polish lightly.

For the second one, melt 1/2 cup ceresin wax and 2 tablespoons yellow beeswax in the top of a double boiler. Take off heat and slowly stir in 2 1/8 cups turpentine and 1 tablespoon pine oil. Cool and pour into containers. Apply with a cloth and let dry. This will need a bit more polishing than the first one.

Beeswax, by the way, is a yellowish-buff color in its natural state as it comes from the hive. You can also buy white beeswax, which has been bleached, and which is generally a little more expensive. They both have the same characteristics, so it's more economical to use the yellow when color is not important.

4. *Wood Floor Nonslip Wax*

The acacia, also called gum arabic, in this mixture is available in drugstores, usually in the form of white powder or flakes. The remaining ingredients are normally carried in hardware or paint stores. Strictly speaking, this is not a wax, but it is a good finish for a wood floor due to the acacia, which provides more friction than a wax finish. This gives it its nonslip character.

Start with 2 cups denatured alcohol, and into this mix 1/2 cup orange shellac, 2 tablespoons acacia, and 2 tablespoons turpentine. Stir until the acacia is dissolved, then put in containers. Apply with a cloth or sponge mop and allow to dry for at least one-half hour. (Note: Denatured alcohol, shellac, and turpentine are flammable.)

5. *Wood Floor Paste Wax*

A paste wax contains more and harder wax than can be put into a liquid form and, consequently, gives one of the best and hardest finishes. Ceresin and montan waxes are derived from minerals, beeswax is of course a secretion of those insects that also make honey, and carnauba wax is a plant product. All waxes, in fact most of the ingredients here, are flammable and should be handled with reasonable caution around the stove.

Put 2 tablespoons yellow beeswax, 5 tablespoons ceresin wax, 9 tablespoons carnauba wax, and 3 tablespoons montan wax together in the top of a double boiler and melt. Separately mix 2 cups mineral spirits, 4 tablespoons turpentine, and 1 tablespoon pine oil. With the heat off, stir this mixture into the melted wax. With a thermometer check the temperature until it cools down to 135° F., which is just above the point at which it will solidify. Then pour into containers (tin containers are best; glass might break, plastic might melt) and leave undisturbed overnight at room temperature. Apply with a cloth or sponge and polish with a clean dry cloth or an electric buffer. If you use an electric buffer, allow to dry for at least one-half hour before polishing.

6. *Linoleum Polish*

For keeping any linoleum surface shiny, melt 1/2 cup carnauba wax, 2 tablespoons paraffin wax and 4 tablespoons yellow beeswax in the top of a double boiler. Remove from heat and stir in 4 cups turpentine, cool, and bottle. Apply a light coat to the linoleum, let dry, and polish with a dry cloth.

7. *Floor Sweeping Compound*

From time to time we are faced with the job of cleaning up a fairly dusty area—the summer cabin after it has been long empty, or part of the house after some remodeling when there is a lot of plaster dust or other remains about. Perhaps you have wished you had some of that sawdust sweeping compound that janitors use, but have never seen it in smaller quantities than thirty-gallon drums. Well, it's actually quite easy to mix up small batches of it if you have some sawdust. If you don't, any lumberyard should be happy to let you have a bucketful for free.

First, roughly sift the sawdust to get out any large chunks of wood or bits of wire or other scratchy material that might be in it. Then take 12 cups of sawdust mixed with 4 cups of rock salt, and stir in 3 cups of mineral oil. Stir until all the oil is absorbed. Sprinkle this on the floor and sweep it up. It will keep down the dust so you won't have to clean the furniture again after you've swept. It can be used over several times until it becomes either too dirty or too dry. (Note: This is a combustible mixture. Keep in a sealed can.)

8. *Floor Mop Oil*

If your job is not so heavy as to require sweeping up, and all you have to do is get the dust bunnies out of the corners, a perfect mop oil can be made by adding one part turpentine to two parts mineral oil. Use it as you would any mop oil by pouring a small amount on the mop just to dampen it so it will pick up the dust. (Note: Turpentine is flammable.)

9. *Waterproofing Concrete*

A concrete garden wall, foundation, or floor which is likely to become wet repeatedly can be waterproofed by mixing 1 1/4 pounds of ammonium stearate into 4 gallons of hot water, and applying two coats of this with a large brush such as those used for house painting. The ammonium stearate is a waxlike material which disperses readily in hot water, and can be found through a chemical supply company.

10. Concrete Cleaner

If you have an old concrete floor, such as in a garage, that is stained and dirty, an easy cleaner is made by mixing together 3 1/4 cups sodium metasilicate, 3/4 cup trisodium phosphate, and 1/2 cup soda ash. Wet down the surface you are cleaning, sprinkle this mixture over it, let it stand for about fifteen minutes and rinse well.

11. Concrete Dustproofer

An untreated concrete floor, especially an old one, seems to grow dust. This is because even a fairly smooth concrete surface is slightly abrasive, and whenever you walk on it, it cuts minute particles of shoe leather from your soles, and tiny bits of the concrete itself are worn away. So, after cleaning it, if it needs it, you might want to give it a finish that will make it both easier to keep clean and smoother and less abrasive, hence less dusty.

Mix 1 quart sodium silicate into 4 quarts of water, mop or brush onto the floor, and allow to dry for at least 24 hours. Sodium silicate is also known as waterglass. It's what grandma used to store eggs in because it seals the pores in the eggshells, preventing oxygen from getting in. It is a rather old-fashioned material, but should be available through most drugstores or chemical supply houses.

12. Tile and Household Cleaner

If you've ever been slightly disappointed, as I have, by that fancy "Miracle Tile Cleaner—Super Grease Cutter—Fast Stain Remover—No Work Polish" that comes in a pretty can or bottle, and regretted the dollar or more you spent on it at the supermarket, you should give trisodium phosphate (TSP) a try. It is available in paint and hardware stores and is a great cleaning agent.

Mix 2 tablespoons in 2 quarts of warm water to clean tile with a sponge or brush. This is also good for painted surfaces, wood-work, door jambs and so on. Use stronger concentrations for heavier cleaning, but be careful; if the solution is too strong it will begin to remove the paint. With the concentration suggested above, it does not require rinsing, but with stronger concentrations it is best to rinse with clear water.

13. Marble Cleaning Powder

For cleaning any marble surface, steps, floors, table tops and so on, mix three parts sodium sulfate with one part sodium sulfite. These are both white powder or crystals. Sprinkle this on a damp cloth or sponge and rub over the area you are cleaning. The very gentle abrasive and cleaning action of this powder will remove stains and grime. Rinse with a swipe of your cloth wrung out in clear water.

14. Carpet Cleaner

Besides using those fancy and expensive solutions that come whoosh-foaming out of those fancy and expensive aerosol cans, there are several other ways to spot clean carpets. One old-fashioned way to remove oil or road grease tracked accidentally into your living room is to cover the spots with cornstarch, leave for one hour, and sweep up.

Another more versatile cleaner can be made by mixing 3 cups of whole wheat flour into a paste with about 1 1/4 cups water. This paste should be more fluid than bread dough but not watery, so you can adjust the proportions to get the right consistency. Then add 1 tablespoon each of aluminum stearate and salicylic acid, and finally stir in 1 1/2 cups mineral oil. Rub this preparation into the area to be cleaned, let it stand for ten or fifteen minutes, wipe away with clear water, and let dry. The drying can be speeded up by vacuuming or brushing to raise the nap.

15. Mineral Oil Emulsion for Tile Floors

One of the most beautiful and durable flooring materials in existence is that large, dark red tile that comes in several versions and is variously known as quarry tile, Spanish tile or padre tile. With proper care it has a deep, warm brown-red color and is remarkably easy to keep clean. In fact, durability and easy maintenance are two strong recommendations which, in my mind, offset the high initial cost of this type of floor. All you need ever do to it is mop it with a mineral oil solution from time to time. We have an old tile floor that was badly worn and discolored and was brought back to life and a beautiful uniform color by rubbing it lightly with straight mineral oil. To make the mineral oil go further, and for routine application once the floor is in good condition, an emulsion can be made by heating 4 cups mineral oil, 3 cups water and 6 tablespoons ammonium oleate in a double boiler. When it gets warm, blend with an egg beater until a whitish emulsion of uniform consistency and color forms, cool, and store it in a jar.

FURNITURE CARE, AND SOME OTHER TREATMENTS FOR WOOD
(For care of leather furniture, see Shoes and Leather.*)*

Whether you have Salvation Army castoffs, Danish modern, American modern, priceless antiques, or rebuilt orange crates, taking a bit of care with the finish from time to time not only preserves the particular beauty of your furniture, but prolongs its useful life. The lustrous glow of a nicely finished piece of wood seems to have a universal appeal. And it doesn't have to be a fancy wood like teak, rosewood, or cocabola. A smooth, satiny finish on a stick of plain old pine or redwood seems to invite touching and produce a warm comfortable feeling in the human psyche. And when you are responsible for that finish, the satisfaction is that much greater.

1. Furniture Finishing Polish

This finishing polish is primarily for the final touch after that last coat of lacquer or whatever goes on a new or refinished piece of furniture, but it is also useful for taking some of the unevenness off an old finish which is cracked or wrinkled. It won't take out all the unevenness, and if you want a perfectly smooth finish you will have to strip the old off and start fresh, but if it's not too bad and you don't want to go the whole way with it, this will help.

To 1 cup turpentine mixed with 1 cup mineral oil, add 1 tablespoon rottenstone powder, stirring in well. Rottenstone is a light gray powder available in paint and hardware stores. Apply to a cloth and rub with medium pressure evenly and with the grain. (Note: Turpentine is flammable.)

The next four are variations on a theme. The purpose is to supply oil to the finish and the wood to keep it from drying out, cracking, and wrinkling, to keep it clean and polished. You might pick out the one you prefer, or experiment with all four.

2. Furniture Lemon Oil Polish

If you enjoy this citrus fragrance, pick up a bottle of lemon oil from the drugstore and mix 1 tablespoon into 1 quart of mineral oil. Plastic spray bottles are good containers for this. Spray it on and wipe clean with a dry cloth.

3. Furniture Wax Polish

As we have said before, carnauba wax is a plant product, and is one of the best, hardest waxes there is. Put 1 tablespoon of carnauba wax in the top of a double boiler with 2 cups of mineral oil and heat until the wax is completely melted into the oil. Allow to cool and put in containers. Wipe on with a cloth, let dry for a few minutes, and polish with a soft dry cloth.

4. Furniture Silicone Polish

For this one just mix 1 tablespoon of silicone oil into 2 cups of mineral oil. The silicone oil will provide a very smooth, glossy surface. If you can't find it at a drugstore, try a foundry or a foundry supply store. It is often sprayed on the inside of molds to facilitate the release of the molded material.

5. Furniture Thin Film Polish

Mix 1 cup benzene into 1/2 cups mineral oil. Keep this in closed containers and handle with care as it is a flammable mixture. Simply wipe on with a soft cloth. (Note: Benzene is flammable and toxic by prolonged inhalation.)

6. Furniture Water Emulsion Polish

Mix together 1 1/4 cups mineral oil, 1 tablespoon distilled pine oil, and 4 tablespoons liquid detergent, stirring until the solution is clear. Then, very slowly, drop by drop at first and stirring constantly, add 1 1/2 cups water. Because of the detergent, which is a wetting agent, the water will mix with the oil forming an emulsion. Apply with a soft cloth, and dry and polish with another cloth immediately.

7. Alcohol Resistant Finish for Wood

This is a finish to use on bare wood. It will penetrate deeper into the wood than other types of finish, so scratches don't bother it and it resists water and alcohol beautifully.

Mix 1 tablespoon of vinegar into 3 cups of paraffin oil. Make sure it is well mixed in. Apply to a cloth and rub into the wood with the grain. Saturate the wood surface well so it can fill pores and soak in. Wipe off excess with a dry cloth afterwards. Let it dry overnight and apply again. The more coats you can give it the better the finish will be, letting it stand overnight between each coat.

8. *Removing Water Spots from Furniture*

Water spots on a finish show as white or light-colored hazy marks, usually rings where a glass has been resting. To remove them, mix 10 drops lemon oil in 2 cups denatured alcohol (any type). Dampen one corner of a soft cloth with this and lightly rub the spots, drying immediately with the dry end of your cloth. (Note: Denatured alcohol is flammable.)

9. *Fireproofing Wood*

This can be used in buildings, on outdoor furniture, camping equipment, on the wood that you use to furnish your camping vehicle, or anywhere it is important to retard the progress of a fire. Nearly anything will burn if exposed to enough heat for enough time, and this preparation will not make it impossible for the wood to burn, but it will make it hard for it to catch.

Into 2 quarts of water, mix 1/2 cup zinc chloride, 1/4 cup ferric chloride, 3 tablespoons boric acid, and 3 tablespoons ammonium phosphate. Spray or brush on two or three coats.

10. *Termite Proofing*

Paradichlorobenzene, otherwise known as moth crystals, does the work here. Dissolve by stirring 1 cup paradichlorobenzene in 8 cups denatured alcohol (any type). Brush on two coats, applying liberally so that it soaks in well. A fairly strong odor remains, so it is primarily for outdoor use. Be careful to use in a well-ventilated area, as the vapors can be irritating. (Note: Paradichlorobenzene is slightly toxic and denatured alcohol is flammable.)

11. Mildewproofing

This is good protection for the north side of the old cabin in a damp climate, or wherever mildew is a problem. Mix together 2 cups copper naphthenate, 1/4 cup amyl acetate, and 3/4 cup zinc bromide. The amyl acetate smells like bananas. It can be obtained from industrial chemical suppliers. The other two, copper naphthenate and zinc bromide, should be available through a drugstore, or the same industrial supplier. Make a dilution of 1/4 cup of that mixture in 1 gallon of water and brush or spray on wood, painted wood, canvas awnings, or other outdoor materials subject to mildew. (Note: Copper naphthenate can be a fire hazard and amyl acetate is flammable and toxic.)

12. Waterproofing Canvas

To keep the drips from coming through tents, awnings, and camping equipment, mix 3 cups of soybean oil with 1 1/2 cups turpentine. Paint on and let dry. This is fairly inexpensive and very easy for waterproofing. It is also beneficial to the canvas, so, after hard use or a year or so of outdoor exposure, depending on the climate, another application is a good idea. (Note: Turpentine is flammable and toxic.)

DISHWASHING HELP

Unless you have maids and butlers or eat all your meals in restaurants, washing up the dishes, along with the next topic, doing the laundry, ranks right up there with floor cleaning as one of the universal tasks. Literally millions of dollars each year are spent on products which people hope will make these things easier and faster, and millions more are spent in advertising to convince you that indeed they will. Until someone invents the ultimate dishwasher, here are some ideas to help you avoid paying an arm and a leg for what you need.

1.   Dishwasher Detergent

A standard detergent to use in dishwashing machines is made by mixing together 2 cups sodium metasilicate, 1 cup soda ash, and 1 cup trisodium phosphate. Use 1/4 cup for each dishwasher load.

2.   Liquid Detergent for Dishwashing

Use 2 or 3 teaspoons of this mixture in your dishpan or sinkful of hot water. Sift or stir together 3 cups trisodium phosphate (TSP) and 1 cup sodium metaphosphate. This softens hard water and will not leave waterspots on the glassware.

3.   Water Softener for Dishes or Laundry

If you are plagued by hard water, either use the previous detergent, or put 1/2 teaspoon or less of the following in your dish or laundry water. Mix well 1 cup sodium metaphosphate, 1 cup sodium metasilicate, and 1/2 cup trisodium phosphate.

4.   Bottle and Jar Cleaner

If you are into home canning or brewing, you will need to wash and sterilize your containers thoroughly before filling them. If you mix 1 teaspoon sodium aluminate and 5 tablespoons caustic soda into 1 gallon hot water and wash your bottles or jars well using a bottle brush, they will be ready for the beans or the brew. Be careful when handling the caustic soda; it is, of course, caustic and can cause skin burns.

The Formula Book

MEMOS

LAUNDRY HELP

What was said above about dishwashing applies even more to washing clothes. More money is spent purchasing laundry aids, and, as any typical day of watching television advertisements will show you, an enormous amount of money is spent in advertising them.

1. *Laundry Detergent*

This is a low-sudsing, biodegradable detergent. Mix thoroughly 3 3/4 cups lauryl pyridinium chloride, 2 1/2 cups sodium dodecylbenzene sulfate, 10 1/2 cups sodium tripolyphosphate, and 8 cups sodium bicarbonate. This last is the well-known baking soda, and the others, despite their long names, are available through drug companies or chemical suppliers. Use as you do most laundry detergents, about one cup per average top-loading washer load.

2. *Additive for Heavily Soiled Laundry*

Mix together well 5 cups mason sand and 3 cups soda ash, and use one or two tablespoons for each load. This small amount provides a scrubbing action which increases the cleaning power of any detergent, especially for heavily soiled work clothes.

3. *Laundry Bleach*

This is a chlorine bleach made with chlorinated lime, which is sometimes called bleaching powder, and is available through hardware or building supply stores. When it is mixed with water it forms chlorine, so the fumes from this should be avoided while you are mixing it.

Into 1 gallon water, mix 2 cups chlorinated lime and 3 cups

sodium carbonate. Stir well, allow the mixture to stand for twenty-four hours, and strain through cheesecloth into bottles with tight caps. Use as you would a commercial bleach, about 1 cup or less to a load of laundry. (Caution: Chlorinated lime can cause burns.)

4. Laundry Bluing

If you have dabbled in watercolor or oil painting, you will know that a small amount of blue added to white will make the white appear whiter, a small amount of red will make it yellower. It is a strange cultural trait of ours that our white sheets and towels are supposed to be as dazzlingly white as we can possibly get them, and one way to do this has traditionally been to add a bit of blue dye to the wash water.

Use 1/4 teaspoon ultramarine blue, 1 3/4 cups sodium bicarbonate, and 1/2 cup corn syrup. Mix well with a spoon or a fork, and use 1/2 teaspoon or less per washer load. Do not put directly on clothes as it is a dye; put it into the water.

5. Laundry Starch

Because of the fancy no-iron "miracle" fabrics that most of our clothes are made of these days, many people have almost forgotten about starching and ironing. However, if we are reading the signs correctly, things will soon start 'o change; we will stop using so much synthetic fabric and go back to cotton, linen, and wool. Many synthetic fabrics are made from petroleum, a nonrenewable resource, require large amounts of energy in their manufacture, and are mostly non-biodegradable. Cotton, linen, wool, silk, and the like are not made from nonrenewable resources, require relatively little energy in their manufacture and processing, and their components may be readily assimilated in the soil when they rot. They have the one, almost ridiculously minor, drawback that they must be ironed to be wrinkle free. By some brilliant accident in the dim, forgotten past, it was found that starch makes the ironing much easier, so . . .

Mix together one part wheat starch and two parts cornstarch, and dissolve 2 teaspoons of the mixture in 1 cup of water. Put this in a plastic spray bottle, and spray on just before you iron.

6.   Fabric Softener

To make diapers, sheets, cotton underwear, etc. baby-soft, mix together 4 cups lauryl pyridinium chloride, 1 cup denatured alcohol (type 40) or isopropyl alcohol and 1/3 cup water. Keep in covered jar or bottle, and add about two tablespoons to the rinse water.

7.   Perspiration Stain Remover

Some people perspire more heavily than others, but we all do to some degree, and it is a very clever and efficient way of controlling temperature. If a shirt or blouse becomes stained, mix 3 tablespoons sodium perborate into 2 cups of water, and apply to a small inconspicuous test area for color-fastness before using on the stain. Saturate the stained area and wash normally.

8.   Mold Stain Remover

Mold and mildew stains can be removed with a mixture of 1 teaspoon of household ammonia and 4 tablespoons hydrogen peroxide in 3/4 cup distilled water. Soak the stain for fifteen minutes or so and flush with clear water. If it is a dark stain repeat the process, then wash normally. (Caution: Do not breath ammonia vapors. Avoid contact of hydrogen peroxide with skin or eyes.)

9. *Rust Stain Remover*

Rust stains are among the most stubborn there are. Mix 3/4 ounce potassium persulfate in 1 pint water, saturate the spot with this, and let it soak for fifteen minutes. Then rinse well with clear water. If it is an especially stubborn stain, repeat the process and wash the garment or fabric in soap and water. (Note: Potassium persulfate can be a fire hazard in concentrated amounts.)

SHOES AND LEATHER

Leather—the processed skins of animals, chiefly cattle—is an extremely useful, beautiful, and durable material. It is still used for footwear, saddles, baseball gloves, and such, for the excellent reason that no synthetic material has been found that will perform satisfactorily as a substitute. Its chief enemies, as with your own skin, are excessive moisture and dryness. You naturally produce oil to keep your own skin in good condition, but leather has been removed from its original owner, and this function is no longer performed for it from the inside; so we must provide the oil from the outside to keep it in condition.

The best leather preservative there is is neat's-foot oil. I used to think that this was oil from the foot of the neat, quite possibly a smallish animal rather like a gerbil. I was disappointed to learn that it is made from the hooves and shins of cattle. Another childhood fantasy lost to education.

1. *Leather Preservative*

Mix equal parts of neat's-foot oil and mineral or castor oil.

For better penetration of the leather, this should be warmed before you rub it on with a cloth. This is a good occasional treatment, every six months or so, for all leather articles such as shoes, belts, clothing, and furniture, except those made of suede.

2.   *Saddle Soap*

It is also a good idea to give leather a thorough cleaning from time to time, before the oil is applied. For this purpose a special soap that contains a lot of oil should be used.

Heat 3 1/2 cups water to a simmer, and slowly add 3/4 cup soap powder, but *not* detergent. Don't stir too hard as it should not be sudsy. Separately, heat 1/4 cup neat's-foot oil and 1/2 cup beeswax or paraffin in the top of a double boiler until the wax melts. Turn off all heat, slowly add the oil and wax to the soapy water, and stir gently until it begins to thicken. Then pour into containers and allow to cool. Using a wet sponge, rub a small amount of this soap into the leather and dry with a clean cloth or towel. (Note: Neat's-foot oil is flammable.)

3.   *Waterproofing Leather*

For outdoor use, especially for shoes and boots, here are two methods of waterproofing, the first is a neat's-foot oil preparation, the second uses silicone oil.

Heat together in a double boiler 2 1/2 ounces neat's-foot oil, 3/4 ounce mineral oil, and 1/2 ounce tallow. Stir gently until well mixed, cool and bottle. Rub into shoes and boots with a cloth.

For the second one, if you can't find Stoddard solvent at the hardware or the drugstore, you might ask at a dry cleaning shop. Mix 1 tablespoon of silicone oil into 1 cup of Stoddard solvent, and apply liberally. (Note: Neat's-foot oil and tallow are flammable.)

GENERAL CLEANING AND POLISHING

Here is a small grab bag of things you can make for various cleaning jobs around the house, ending with a set of polishes for different kinds of metal.

1. Disinfectant

This is a general disinfectant that can be used anywhere in the house. All of the ingredients are available from a good drugstore or a chemical supplier.

Warm, but do not boil, 1 1/4 cups cresylic acid, and stir in 3 tablespoons oleic acid. Separately mix 1 teaspoon caustic soda into 1/2 cup water and add this to the first mixture. Then add 2/3 cup sulfonated castor oil and mix well. Use full strength or diluted in water, depending on the job. Exercise caution in handling the caustic soda.

2. Ammonia Cleaning Powder

Ammonia helps cut through grease and wax, and this combination is an excellent general cleaner. Mix equal parts of powdered soap and ammonium carbonate, and add two tablespoons or more of this to one quart of warm water.

3. Household Ammonia

For straight ammonia, mix 3/4 cup ammonium hydroxide into 1 gallon of water. The ammonium hydroxide is a highly concentrated liquid which can cause burns and has strong, irritating vapors, so it should be handled with caution, and the utensils used in measuring it should be thoroughly rinsed.

4. Household Ammonia Substitute

If you don't like the smell of ammonia, here is a mixture that has roughly the same cleaning characteristics. Into 1 gallon water, mix 6 tablespoons trisodium phosphate and 1/2 tablespoon lauryl pyridinium chloride. This can be used full strength for heavy cleaning, or diluted with equal amounts of water.

5. Wall and Woodwork Cleaner

Into 1 quart hot water, mix 4 ounces corn flour, 1/2 ounce copper sulfate, and 1/8 teaspoon alum. Apply to walls, cupboards, and woodwork with a sponge or cloth.

6. Drain Cleaner

Mix together 1 cup baking soda, 1 cup salt, and 1/4 cup cream of tartar. Once a week or so put 1/4 cup down the drain followed by a cup of boiling water, and flush with cold water. This will keep the drains free and prevent odors.

7. Drain Opener

If a drain is persistently sluggish or clogged this mixture can be used, but care should be taken not to allow it to come in contact with the skin, as it is highly caustic. All of these ingredients can be obtained from a hardware or building supply store. Mix together 3 cups caustic potash, 1 cup calcium carbonate (chalk) and 3/4 cup caustic soda. Keep in airtight containers. Pour 2 tablespoons in the drain followed by a cup of hot water. Let stand for thirty minutes, and flush with cold water. (Caution: Caustic potash and caustic soda can be irritants to the skin and can cause burns.)

8. Glass Spray Cleaner

An excellent glass and window cleaner is made by mixing 1 cup of denatured alcohol or isopropyl alcohol into 2 cups of water, and adding 5 drops of lactic acid, which can be found in grocery or hardware and paint stores. This works well in spray bottles.

9. *Glass Scratch Remover*

Iron oxide, also called jeweler's rouge or polishing rouge, is a very fine, dark red powder, which you can get at hobby shops or jewelry supply stores. Mix 1 ounce of iron oxide into a paste with 1 ounce of glycerin and 1 ounce of water. This mixture will remove superficial scratches from a glass tabletop, mirror, window, or whatever, if you put a small amount on a cloth and rub the scratched area, washing off with clear water from time to time to check your progress. If the scratches are quite deep it will take a while.

10. *Hand Cleaner for Grease and Grime*

Mix together 1 cup mineral oil and 1/4 cup diglycol laurate. Rub a small amount on hands to remove grease, grime, paint, ink, and the like. Rinse with plain water.

11. *Metal Cleaner*

A simple, all-purpose metal polish can be made by mixing 3 cups soda ash, 3/4 cup trisodium phosphate (TSP), and 1 1/4 cups baking soda. Rub this on with a damp cloth and rinse clean. The soda ash and TSP are available in paint and hardware stores.

12. *Metal Polish*

An all-purpose metal polish can be made by mixing together 1 cup diatomaceous earth, a white powder available from swimming pool supply dealers, 1/2 cup household ammonia, and 1/2 cup denatured alcohol. Add just enough water to this to obtain the consistency of thick cream. Shake well before using, and apply with a soft cloth, rubbing well. Rinse off with water and dry. (Note: Use caution in handling household ammonia. Denatured alcohol is flammable.)

38

13. Aluminum Cleaner

To clean a stained aluminum pot, toy, piece of sculpture, or automotive equipment, mix 2 tablespoons powdered alum into 1 cup of trisodium phosphate, and add just enough water to form a thick paste. Dip a soft cloth into the paste and rub on the aluminum. Rinse off with water.

14. Aluminum Polish

To give aluminum a high polish, take 3/4 cup chalk (also called whiting) and mix in 1/2 cup powdered alum and 1/2 cup talc. Dip a damp cloth in this mixture and rub the aluminum. Rinse with water and dry with a soft cloth.

15. Brass Polish

This paste polish goes to town on doorknobs, boat fittings and what have you. Petroleum distillate is a colorless liquid, available from an oil company or service station. First mix 3/4 tablespoon stearic acid into 1/4 cup petroleum distillate. Then add 1/2 tablespoon caustic soda, and 1 tablespoon denatured alcohol. Mix in enough talc to make a paste. Apply this with a soft cloth and wipe clean. (Note: Caustic soda is an irritant to the skin and can cause burns. Petroleum distillate and denatured alcohol are flammable.)

16. Silver Polish

First, here's an old method of cleaning stained silver. Place it in a pan and cover with sour milk. Let it stand overnight, and rinse off in cold water. This may sound old-fashioned and strange, but it does work quite well.

A more modern type of silver cleaner and polish is the paste type, which is made by heating 1 1/2 cups water and 2 tablespoons stearic acid in the top of a double boiler until the stearic acid melts. Then turn off the heat and add 1/2 teaspoon soda ash, 1/2 teaspoon trisodium phosphate, and 1 cup diatomaceous earth, stirring into a paste. Allow to cool and put in containers. This is applied with a soft cloth, rubbed, and washed off with warm water.

17. Gold Polish

Gold seldom needs polishing, as it doesn't tarnish, but if it just sits around for a long time it does get dirty and may become scratched, so here is a polish to keep your ingots looking fresh and to brighten up your watches, rings, and other jewelry. Fuller's earth is a very fine powder which can be obtained from building supply or ceramic supply stores. Take 1/2 cup Fuller's earth, 1/2 cup chalk (calcium carbonate), 1 tablespoon ammonium sulfate, and 1 teaspoon aluminum powder, and mix with a fork. Using a damp cloth, pick up a small amount of this mixture and rub it on, cleaning off with a clean dry cloth.

18. Lens Cleaner

This is an excellent cleaner and polisher for the fine lenses in eyeglasses, cameras, telescopes, binoculars, or whatever other optical equipment you may have. Melt 2 tablespoons potassium oleate along with 1 tablespoon glycerin in the top of a double boiler, and then stir in 1/4 teaspoon turpentine. Apply a small amount with a piece of soft cloth such as a square cut from an old T shirt, and polish with a clean piece of the same material. Do not use paper towels; they may feel soft, but their fibers are abrasive and may scratch a finely polished piece of glass. (Note: Turpentine is flammable.)

19. Porcelain Cleaner

This is for cleaning stains from dishes, sinks, and tubs—any porcelain object in fact. Mix together 3/4 cup sodium sulfate and

1/4 cup sodium sulfite. Dip a damp cloth or sponge in this powder, rub it over the area to be cleaned, and rinse with clean water.

20. Upholstery Cleaner

Not for stains, but for general cleaning of home or car upholstery. Mix 4 tablespoons oil (Castile) soap into 3 quarts hot water. Then stir in 1 tablespoon borax, 4 tablespoons glycerin and 2 tablespoons ethylene chloride. Apply this to soiled upholstery with a sponge or cloth and rinse with clean water.

21. Grease Spot Remover

Fuller's earth is a very fine powder which is very adsorptive. To remove grease spots, sprinkle a small amount of Fuller's earth on the spot, brush it in well in all directions, and remove it with a damp cloth.

22. Ink Spot Remover

For ink spills on cloths or upholstery that plain water won't get out, mix 1/2 teaspoon sodium perborate in 1/2 cup water. Soak the spot with this and rinse with a cloth or sponge and clean water.

23. Toilet Bowl Cleaner

Mix together 4 cups sodium bicarbonate and 3/4 cup caustic soda. Store it in an airtight can or jar. To use, sprinkle in the toilet bowl, let stand for about a half-hour, then brush with a long handled toilet brush and flush with clean water. This is quite caustic, so if it gets on your hands or skin wash it off immediately with clean water. (Caution: Caustic soda can cause burns to the skin.)

24. Window Cleaner Spray

If you've ever wondered what's in some of those fancy expensive bottles or cans of window spray you buy, wonder no more. You'll be surprised at the least—and maybe downright mad—at what you've been paying for. Here's a way to make your own at a fraction of the store-bought price.

You'll need some ethylene glycol (this is permanent antifreeze that you get at your service station and use in your radiator, and can be bought in small cans), and some plain tap water. Measure out 3 cups of water and stir in 2 tablespoons of ethylene glycol. Transfer to a plastic spray bottle, spray glass, and wipe off with a lint-free cloth.

FIRES IN THEIR PLACES AND OUT OF THEM

Fires in their places are wonderful things. Out of their places, they range from mildly annoying to fully catastrophic. In their places, they warm us in winter, cook our food, burn our tobacco, and serve a million other useful and comfortable purposes. Unwanted fires can cause unpleasant odors, as when a fire accidentally starts in a wastebasket, or can destroy houses, whole cities, and vast areas of beautiful forest, causing at the same time much suffering and death to human and animal populations.

Combustion is a curious process, and what happens when a piece of wood burns might be of some interest.

First, combustion is a chemical reaction in which different elements combine with oxygen, and, in the process of combining, release energy. For example, when carbon burns, it is combining with oxygen to form carbon dioxide (CO_2), and when hydrogen burns it is combining with oxygen to form water (H_2O), of course in vapor form. In each case, the combining releases definite amounts of energy which we know as heat and light.

A piece of dry wood is roughly 20 percent water; when it

burns this water turns to vapor. It also contains very small amounts of mineral elements which are left as ash when a piece of wood has burned completely. The wood is mostly, roughly 80 percent, cellulose. The cellulose molecule is a long, complex string made up of thousands of carbon, hydrogen, and oxygen atoms. In the presence of a sufficient amount of heat for a sufficient length of time, from an already burning match, gas flame, overheating electrical wire, or a bolt of lightning, the molecules at the outer edge of the wood become more and more agitated and vibrate faster and faster until they begin breaking apart. When this happens, the individual carbon, hydrogen, and oxygen atoms come apart and fly out of the wood by the millions. They then rearrange themselves in hundreds of different ways. A carbon atom may combine with two oxygen atoms, releasing energy and forming carbon dioxide. Two hydrogen atoms may combine with one oxygen atom, releasing energy and forming water vapor. One carbon atom and four hydrogen atoms can combine to form methane, natural gas, which in turn will burn, combining with oxygen, releasing energy, and forming carbon dioxide and water vapor.

Besides the oxygen atoms coming out of the breaking cellulose, there are oxygen atoms in the surrounding air. When the air in the immediate vicinity of the fire is heated it expands, becomes lighter, and rises. As it rises, cool air moves in from the sides to take its place, and we have a draft, lifting the results of combustion, all that carbon dioxide and water vapor, away, and bringing in a fresh supply of oxygen to combine with the carbon and hydrogen and keep the fire burning.

Among the many compounds formed by various combinations of carbon and hydrogen atoms are pentane, hexane, heptane, and octane, which are the components of gasoline. A burning piece of wood is rather like a small refinery.

If the fire is large enough, the water vapor that is created may be lifted high enough to cool and condense into visible water droplets. This is what causes the cloud one can sometimes see forming over a forest fire, a burning field, or a burning dump.

With that introduction, here are some ways to start fires, as well as to stop them.

1. Fireplace Starter

If you have forgotten your Boy Scout techniques, here is a way to get the logs burning in the fireplace without messing with papers and kindling. Simply mix 5 pounds sawdust with 1 quart fuel oil, or oil from your car if you change it yourself. Allow one hour for complete absorption, and store it in airtight containers. Sprinkle this mixture around some small logs or split pieces of larger ones and light. (Caution: The mixture of sawdust and oil is flammable.)

2. Charcoal Lighter

As with so many things, when you buy charcoal lighter liquid in a can from the grocery store, it comes under the heading of "How to Spend a Lot of Money for Something Very Simple." They may use deodorized kerosene, or put a small bit of perfume in the mixture, but once the coals are ready for cooking, the kerosene is thoroughly burned off and leaves no odor. If you do want to deodorize the kerosene, see number 4 below. Mix 1/4 cup kerosene into 2 3/4 cups mineral oil. Store in airtight containers. Pour over the charcoal, allow to penetrate for a minute, and light. (Note: Kerosene is flammable and toxic.)

3. Alcohol Solid Fuel

This is what some people call canned heat, so you will want some suitable containers for it; empty film cans with screw-on lids would be one idea. Dissolve 1/8 cup stearic acid into 1 cup denatured alcohol, and separately dissolve 1 1/2 teaspoons caustic soda in 1 cup denatured alcohol—that's 2 cups of denatured alcohol used separately. Then heat both mixtures to 140° F., and mix them together. Pour into cans, let cool, and put on the lids. These can be used under the chafing dish or fondue pot and are

44

handy for camping and picnics. (Please do not leave the burned out containers on the countryside. Take them home and reuse them.) (Caution: Caustic soda can cause burns to skin. Denatured alcohol is flammable.)

4. Oil for Lamps and Torches

If you like the soft, warm glow of an oil lamp, or the dramatic effect of outdoor torches, but can't stand the smell of kerosene, read on. Put 3 ounces of lime into 1 gallon of kerosene, and stir thoroughly for a couple of minutes. Strain through several layers of cheesecloth to remove the bits of lime, and there you are. If you want to get fancy and have a lamp with a clear glass reservoir, you might mix a few drops of an oil-base dye in with it, or a few drops of oil-base flavoring, for a scent thrill. Choice of color and/or smell is yours. (Note: Kerosene is flammable and toxic.)

5. Firewood Substitute

There are at least two useful things that can be done with old newspapers; they can be recycled to make new paper, or they can be made into "logs" to burn in the fireplace. It is said that, if you cut your own firewood, a good log will warm you twice, once in the cutting and once in the burning. The same might be said of newspapers, they can warm you the first time when you read of the idiocies humans perpetrate on one another, and a second time when you burn them. Paper is, after all, just a thin sheet of wood fibers, so if you roll a bunch of paper up, you have something approximating a piece of wood again.

First, mix up a batch of library glue (listed under *Miscellaneous Home Goodies*). Add a little more water to make it thin enough to paint it on with a brush. Separate a stack of newspapers into single sheets leaving them folded down the center the way they normally come. Take a round stick, such as a broomstick, and coat it well with wax so it will slide out of the center of the roll when you have finished. Then, using a small brush, dab some paste on the top of a sheet of newspaper and roll it tightly around the stick. Dab each sheet and roll it up until the roll is about 4 inches in diameter. It doesn't matter how you dab the paste on the paper, in a big X, down the sides and across the top, or in several random spots here and there, just don't do it the same for each sheet or the layers of paste in the same places will begin to make lumps. Secure the roll with tape or large rubber bands until the paste is dry, and remove the stick. If you use masking tape to hold the roll together you can just leave it on and burn it with the log.

6.   Fire Extinguisher

Putting out fires is perhaps more important than starting them, and for quickly dousing the occasional grease fire in the kitchen, nothing surpasses that wonderful and many-talented substance, bicarbonate of soda. We keep an extra box in the cupboard for just that purpose. Sprinkled over a blazing broiler, it snuffs a fire quickly and with minimal mess. Often, the steak can be salvaged by rinsing it off and it is still edible.

For a more versatile and heavy-duty liquid fire extinguisher, make a mixture of 2 cups soda ash, available from paint and hardware stores, 1 cup alum, 3/4 cup borax, 1/4 cup potash, available from feed and grain stores or chemical distributors, and 3 pints sodium silicate (waterglass). Mix until the dry ingredients are dissolved in the waterglass, and use 3 cups of this in a gallon of water. Using a spray can with a fairly high volume coarse spray, direct at the base of a fire.

7.   Fireproofing Cloth

To fireproof clothes, awnings, tents, banners, and other textiles, soak them in a solution of 1 cup ammonium chloride, and 1/2 cup ammonium phosphate in 3 pints water. Soak well and let dry.

For fireproofing wood, see the formula under *Furniture Care.*

46

8. Fireproofing Christmas Trees

The electric light has replaced the candle as a Christmas tree decoration. This is unfortunate, as the tree lit by the soft glow of candles is an unforgettably beautiful part of Christmas Eve tradition. Of course, there is good reason; with candles burning on the tree, the fire hazard is great. If you do use them on your tree, be sure to check that your city fire regulations allow the use of candles. The candles should be placed judiciously, so there is not a branch just above a candle, and of course they must be watched carefully when they are lit and not left burning when no one is in the room. And the tree can be sprayed with, and kept standing in a bucket of, the following mixture.

Into 1 gallon water, mix 1 cup ammonium sulphate, 1/2 cup boric acid, and 2 tablespoons borax. Mix well, spray on the tree, and let the trunk stand in this solution instead of plain water.

This is also a good precaution against fires from the overheating of electric lights.

9. Chimney Soot Remover

Periodic cleanouts used to be done by the chimney sweep, but with his disappearance many people neglect this unpleasant job. As a result their flues stop drawing properly after several years, and they end up with smoky rooms. It really isn't necessary to climb on the roof with a chain and knock all the soot down into the fireplace and get the living room filthy. Just mix 1 cup of salt with 1 cup of zinc oxide powder and sprinkle on a hot fire. This will help keep the flue clean.

CONTROLLING BUGS AND OTHER PESTS

Cockroaches and rats, to name just two pests, have been travelers on this globe for at least as long as, if not longer than, humans. These resourceful and adaptable creatures have managed to accustom themselves to our presence, and live largely off the spoils of our existence; crumbs spilled on the kitchen floor, garbage heaps, and the like. No doubt they all have their place in "The Scheme of Things," and even if we could exterminate them, perhaps we shouldn't. That is why we speak only of control. Even the best run household is invaded from time to time, and not all cockroaches have literary genius, not all ants are viewed primarily as industrious little creatures, and not all rodents, not even their ears, are cute. Mostly they are in our way and we would like to discourage them as houseguests, so here is a smattering of control methods that, used carefully, will not endanger yourself, your children, or your pets at the same time.

1. Cockroach Exterminator

Mix together 4 tablespoons borax, 2 tablespoons flour, and 1 tablespoon cocoa powder. Put it in bottle caps or other small open containers and place them where the cockroaches will run across the mixture and be surprised at the free lunch, only to find that it gives them fatal indigestion.

2. Fly Spray

Into 7 cups deodorized kerosene, mix 1 tablespoon methyl salicylate, and 3/4 cup pyrethrin, stirring until the pyrethrin is dissolved. Use this as a spray, either directly on flies, or on screens and other areas where flies congregate. (Note: Kerosene is flammable and toxic.)

3. Ant Exterminator

This works on ants rather like the cockroach powder does on the roaches. To 1/2 cup molasses, add 1/4 cup sugar and 1/4 cup dry yeast, stirring into a paste. Coat pieces of cardboard with this, and place them in the ant runways.

4. *Bedbug Exterminator*

These little devils are not very common, but they do live on in old mattresses and second-hand furniture. They are also very hard to spot because they prefer the darkness, and will hide instantly at the first suggestion of light. But if you wake up with what you think are mosquito bites, except that you haven't seen or heard any mosquitoes, chances are the bedbugs have been after you. DDT powder works, of course, but the stuff virtually never breaks down, and, if ingested by humans or animals, it gets stored in fatty tissues. Tests have shown that probably everyone in the world has some DDT in him, so if you don't feel like adding more of this remarkable poison to your poor body, make a mixture of 3/4 cup powdered alum, 2 tablespoons powdered boric acid, and 2 tablespoons salicylic acid, and sprinkle this around where you suspect the bugs might be lurking.

5. *Mothproofing*

To protect any washable fabric against moths, mix 1 teaspoon of ammonium selanate into 1 gallon of water, and soak the material in this for a few minutes. Hang up to dry, and the moths will turn up their noses at it.

6. *Mouse and Rat Hole Sealer*

If you've ever tried to keep rats, packrats, or mice out of an area that they wanted to be in, you know it can be quite difficult. They will gnaw through wood, rags, screens, and even tin cans that you stuff in their hole or nail over it. Here is a substance that will stop them, however, and they will either have to call it quits, or find a new access route. They can be quite clever at the latter, too, and you will have to watch carefully for any evidence of reentry.

Thoroughly dissolve 1 1/2 cups asphalt in 1 1/4 cups kerosene, and then stir in 2 cups powdered asbestos until it reaches a putty-like consistency. Using a trowel or broad knife, fill the holes you want to seal up. All of these materials are generally available in a hardware or building supply store. (Note: Kerosene is flammable and toxic. Do not inhale asbestos dust.)

7. An Ingenious Rat Poison

If you want to reduce the rat population without endangering the dogs, cats, and small children in the area, you might see how this works. Rats are omnivorous, and will eat almost anything, while this usually does not appeal to dogs or cats.

Make a mixture of cement and flour, in roughly equal amounts. Set a pan of this dry powder out next to a pan of water. For a hungry rat the results could be astonishing.

PAINTS AND BRUSHES

Everyone knows how to paint. Simply buy a can of the right color and slap it on with brush or roller. The part that most amateur around-the-house painters seem to dislike and neglect is the cleaning up, but this is the part that can save hours of labor and considerable amounts of money on brushes. Most spills can be cleaned immediately as you go along with a cloth carried in the back pocket for that purpose. Stubborn ones may need a little turpentine on the cloth. A well-cared-for brush will last many years, literally until the fibers of the brush are worn down too short to use, so it pays to spend a few minutes after each use cleaning it up instead of letting the caked paint dry out so that it has to be thrown away. So here are a few tips for cleaning brushes, removing paint and varnish, and, finally, a preparation for mildewproofing paint.

1. Softening an Old Brush

First, here is a rather simple and old-fashioned method of reviving a stiff old paint brush. Put the brush in enough boiling vinegar to just cover the bristles and simmer for a few minutes. Wash it out in warm water and soap and then dry.

2. *Paint Brush Cleaner*

If a brush does have old paint dried out in the bristles, here is how to clean it up so it doesn't have to be thrown away. Mix 4 cups kerosene with 2 cups oleic acid, and separately mix 1/4 cup household ammonia with 1/4 cup denatured alcohol. Combine the two mixtures and allow the brushes to soak in this for twelve hours. Then wash them with soap and warm water and dry. (Note: Denatured alcohol and kerosene are flammable and kerosene can be toxic.)

3. *Paint and Varnish Remover*

There are many people who purely and simply enjoy taking an old piece of furniture and repairing or refinishing it to make it useful and beautiful once again; and there are others of us for whom this is not a joy but, because of our limited incomes, a necessity. For removing an old finish, here is a commercial-type product that you can mix in advance and store in an airtight container. To 1 1/2 cups pumice powder, add 2 cups calcium carbonate, 1 cup caustic soda, and 3/4 cup caustic potash. When you are ready to use it, take about 2 cups, more or less, depending on the size of the job you have before you, and add enough water to form a paste the consistency of heavy cream. Brush this on in one direction, allow to work for fifteen minutes, and wash off with water and a stiff brush. Be careful not to get this mixture on your skin, as it is very caustic and can cause burns. If it does get splashed on hands or arms, the best procedure is to wash immediately with plenty of clear water.

4. *Paint Remover*

Here is a somewhat milder and less fearsome way to remove old paint. It is also one of our old-fashioned techniques. Simply brush on our old friend, sodium silicate (waterglass), let it stand

51

for fifteen minutes, and scrape off, washing as you go with a stream of water.

On many older pieces of furniture the finish is very hard or has things mixed in it which we are not used to dealing with, such as blood or milk, and can be the very devil to get off, especially where no sealer was used, many coats are present, and the finish has penetrated down into the wood. In these cases you will need to use several applications and a good sharp scraper.

5. Paint Spot Remover

If there are a few spots that you miss until the whole job is over and they have dried too hard to simply wipe up, mix a small amount of equal parts of turpentine and household ammonia, dip one end of a rag in and this will generally remove the stubborn ones. (Note: Turpentine is flammable and toxic. Avoid vapors of household ammonia.)

6. Mildewproofing Paint

To make paint resistant to mildew and the dry rot that goes with it that can cause you to replace whole sections of your house from time to time, use the following. Into 7 1/2 ounces linseed oil, mix 19 ounces zinc oxide and 1/2 ounce mercuric chloride. Mix to a smooth paste and add to 1 gallon of any oil-base paint, stirring very thoroughly to insure that it is well dispersed through the paint. (Note: Linseed oil is flammable. Mercuric chloride is very toxic by ingestion.)

IN THE KITCHEN

There seems to be much more interest in good cooking now than there was, say, twenty years ago. The television-chef shows have been very successful, even if most people watch them for their humor and drama rather than for any recipes that are offered. This is not altogether a bad thing; that there is humor and drama in cooking is a fact little enough recognized. Indeed, the career of the serious amateur cook could be characterized by a description that might just as easily fit his life. It consists of long periods of time filled with rather ordinary and mostly boring activity, punctuated by black moments of horrible failure on the one hand, and made bearable and even desirable on the other hand, when human frailty is surpassed and creative perfection is achieved. At any rate, if you enjoy messing about in the kitchen, for whatever reasons, here are some not so ordinary things you may enjoy trying out.

1. *Extracts of Special Flavors*

For mixing small amounts of flavoring extracts, by far the easiest way to get ethyl alcohol is to buy a bottle of vodka. Since rather strong flavoring is added to it, the cheapest brand you can get is the best. Remember that ethyl alcohol is the only variety of alcohol that can be taken internally, so don't substitute some other kind.

Mix 1/4 cup ethyl alcohol and 1/4 cup water, and to this add 15 drops almond oil, or whatever other essential oil you wish: lemon, vanilla, strawberry, etc.

2. *Whipped Cream Improver*

If you like to make whipped cream in advance of use, you may have noticed that it will sometimes "leak" a thin skim milk. To prevent this happening, use 1 teaspoon of gelatin for each cup of cream to be whipped. If you use sugar, put a tablespoon or two in at the very end when the cream is stiff, along with a few drops of vanilla extract if you wish.

3. *Jar and Bottle Sealer*

For home canning, in fact for any kind of canning, it is important to have an airtight seal so that airborne bacteria cannot get into the jars and eat whatever you have put up, thus spoiling

53

it before you can eat it. An easy way to effect an airtight seal is to heat 1 cup of water and 1 teaspoon of gelatin in a double boiler until the gelatin is dissolved, and then add 3 tablespoons glycerin, and paint this on the inside of jar or bottle caps with a brush before putting them on.

4. Refrigerator Deodorizer

If your refrigerator is occasionally the receptacle for leftover spaghetti sauce, remnants of garlic cloves, yesterday's sauerbraten, and the catch from last weekend's fishing expedition, it can quickly build up a combination of mutually incompatible odors that will reappear in the butter or the spinach. To keep the refrigerator fresh you can make some odor-absorbing blocks, that can be used over and over again, in the following way. First get some small cardboard boxes, such as matchboxes or paper clip containers, to use as molds. Then mix up 1 cup of Portland cement, 1/4 cup activated charcoal, 1/4 cup calcium carbonate, 1/2 cup vermiculite, and 2 teaspoons powdered aluminum. Add just enough water to achieve the consistency of thick cream and pour this into your molds. Dry the blocks in the oven for twenty-four hours at 200° F., remove them from the molds, and place a couple of them in the refrigerator. They work well for a week or two, after which time they can be reactivated by putting them in the oven set at 350° F. for two hours.

5. Oven Cleaner

Several good oven cleaners are on the market, but they all suffer from one or more of the following objections. Some are caustic and can cause burns, others create fumes not unlike tear gas or mace and will drive you from the house until they dissipate, and they all cost more than they are worth. To clean the oven in a reasonably nontoxic fashion, mix 1 cup sodium perborate, 1/2 cup soda ash, 1/2 cup trisodium phosphate, and 2 tablespoons powdered soap. Apply with a damp sponge or cloth and rinse with clear water.

54

6. *Storing Flour and Cereals*

If you have ever been troubled by bugs in the flour and other cereal products, put a couple of bay leaves in the canisters or tins that you store them in. The bugs don't like the bay leaves and will stay out, and the leaves won't impart any noticeable flavor to the flour.

7. *Growing and Drying Herbs*

Many herbs are weeds which people have found to be tasty. Most of them are very hardy and will grow almost anywhere, and it is a shame to pay seventy-five cents or more for a small bottle of dried leaves when the fresh leaves are so much more flavorful. We have had dill plants which were four feet high, and a basil bush you couldn't kill with a stick. In hot dry climates rosemary thrives. Mint can take a lot of sun but needs a lot of water, and watch out for cats; they love mint almost as much as catnip, which it is related to. To dry your herbs, either break off the main branches or pull the plant up by the roots before the first frost and hang them upside down with a paper bag tied around the leaves. When they are dry you can knock the leaves off inside the bag, break them up a little into small bits, and you will have a year's supply or better of basil or whatever, that will taste at least twice as good as the old store-bought stuff, and it's free.

8. *Storing Spices*

Spices, herbs, coffee, tea, and all those things, should be stored in airtight containers, *away from light*. This means opaque containers, preferably those little tin canisters with a rubber seal around the top. We *know* they are sold in the store mostly in those little clear glass bottles, but, according to our experts, light is the worst enemy of these aromatic plants. So, if you grow your own, and you insist on using those commercial spice bottles to store them in, at least paint them black, and try to keep them in a cool dark place.

9.   *Antacid Liquid*

When indigestion strikes, you don't have to rush out to the drugstore and spend a lot of money for relief. I know you have three of the ingredients in your kitchen right now, and you may even have the fourth. To 1 cup of water, add 1 tablespoon bicarbonate of soda, 1 teaspoon sugar, and 5 drops more or less to taste of peppermint oil. One or two tablespoons of this may soothe the results of your indiscretion. (If symptoms persist see a doctor.)

MISCELLANEOUS HOME GOODIES

What we have here is a potpourri of items that don't quite fit under any of the several headings above. Some are purely fun, some are practical, and some are both.

1.   *Saving Soap*

If you take a good look at that tag end of the soap bar that you are about to throw away because it has become too small to do any good, you will see that it is a not insignificant fraction of the original bar; for most people it is about one-fifth. Which means that if you save it, for every five bars you use you will have a free one. So toss those soap remnants in a box or large jar instead of the wastebasket, and when you have collected enough, cut them up into slivers, put them in a pan with not quite enough water to cover, and boil gently, uncovered, until the whole is reduced by approximately the amount of water you added. Then pour into molds, either cardboard boxes or plastic soap dishes, which can be reused, and allow to cool overnight. Remove from the molds and allow to air dry for at least two weeks. The longer they dry out, the harder they become and the longer they will last.

2. Candles

In recent years candlemaking has become quite a widespread hobby and, for some, who sell the results of their work, a source of additional income. Others have capitalized on the popularity of this hobby by manufacturing kits, and nearly all department stores sell fancy and expensive boxes containing the rudimentary materials for making candles, as well as artsy-craftsy books, with four-color illustrations, on the subject. If you are not after an "art candle," but just want to be able to make something serviceable, nothing could be simpler. Select a paperboard mailing tube of a diameter you think fitting and cut it to the length you desire. (Square candles are easily made using quart milk cartons as molds.) Close one end of the mailing tube mold with a paperboard disc cut to size and taped in place, and pour a little vegetable oil into the tube, tipping it around so that the whole inside surface is coated. For the wicks use cotton wicking, or any string that will burn; the thicker the string the bigger the flame for fat candles, the thinner the string the smaller the flame for skinny candles. Make a small hole in the bottom of your mold, tie a knot in one end of the wick so it won't slip through the hole, and, after the wick is in place, seal the hole with a pinch of clay or putty or something that won't melt at the temperature of molten wax. Tie the top end of the wick to a pencil or matchstick to hold it straight and centered while you pour in the wax. Now melt 2 cups paraffin wax and 1 cup stearic acid into the top of a double boiler, and pour a small amount into the mold to check for leaks around the bottom. If leaks appear, plug them with clay or putty; if not, pour the wax slowly into the mold to the top. As wax cools, it shrinks, and a slight depression may appear in the center around the wick. You can fill this up by pouring in a little more wax. When the wax is cool, simply cut away the paper mold. To get a smooth, shiny surface, hold the candle by the wick and dip it first in boiling water, then in ice water. (See Appendix J for illustrations of procedure.)

3. Luminaries

This is a very attractive and remarkably simple outdoor lighting effect you can achieve with your homemade candles. It originated in Mexico and is used widely throughout the Southwest. For each light take a medium-sized brown paper bag, put two or three inches of sand in it, and push a candle into the sand in the center of the bag. If you carefully fold down the top edge of the bag all around like a cuff, it will hold its shape better. The sand holds the candle upright and extinguishes it when it burns down, the paper bag protects the candle from being blown out by the wind and provides a warm, golden light. Line driveways and walks with them, and use them for parties and festive occasions, especially at Christmas time. There is a certain amount of work involved in shoveling sand into twenty or thirty bags, but the effect is subtly spectacular, if such a combination has meaning, and is well worth the effort.

4. Modeling Clay

Here is a simple, nontoxic modeling clay, edible in small amounts but not tasty, to keep the kids busy on rainy afternoons, or to amuse yourself at odd moments. Mix 1 cup cornstarch with 2 cups bicarbonate of soda and 1 1/2 cups cold water. Add enough food coloring to give the color you desire, if any, and heat over a medium fire, stirring constantly until a dough-like consistency is achieved. Cool, covered with a damp cloth. A coat of shellac will seal and preserve the finished products.

5. Preserving Cut Flowers

If you enjoy brightening up the house with flowers from the garden, here is a way to make them last longer. To 1 cup granulated sugar, add 20 drops silver nitrate, mix well, and add 1 teaspoon to the water the flowers stand in. (Caution: Silver nitrate is poison and may cause burns.)

6. *Book Cover Coating*

To protect those hardbound books that get a lot of wear and tear, such as reference works, mix equal amounts of white shellac and denatured alcohol and paint the covers. Hold the cover open and away from the pages while you do this, because if any shellac gets on the page edges they will stick together. (Note: Shellac and denatured alcohol are flammable.)

7. *Library Glue*

A good liquid glue for our cutting and pasting chores, or the children's art work (or our own), can be made by mixing 4 tablespoons yellow dextrin, 2 tablespoons calcium chloride, and 2 cups water. Mix together at room temperature, then heat slowly while stirring, but do not allow to boil. Cook gently until the consistency of thin syrup has been reached and store in bottles.

8. *Moisture Protection*

Fine equipment of all kinds often comes packaged with a small bag of silica gel. This substance adsorbs moisture, protecting against rust and mildew, and is best used in a fairly well enclosed space such as a box with a lid or a drawer. You can make up your own by simply putting some silica gel crystals in small cheesecloth bags. Activate the crystals by heating in an oven for four or five hours at 400° F. After about a month, depending on the humidity, they will have adsorbed their limit and should be reactivated by heating again in the oven. They can be used over and over in this way indefinitely.

9. *Galvanized Coating Repair*

If the roof of the old shed is starting to rust, you can repair it by first wire brushing over the spot, and then sprinkling a mixture of 1/2 tablespoon powdered zinc, 1/4 tablespoon powdered lead, and 6 tablespoons powdered tin over the area to be redone. Then heat with a blowtorch or a propane torch until the powdered metal melts and flows over the damaged area. Do not keep the torch on it for too long or the repairing compound will become too liquid and, especially if the piece is at an angle, it will run right off the edge. (Note: Powdered lead can cause lead poisoning if taken internally.)

10. *Fuel Improver for Oil Furnaces*

Naphthalene is also called tar camphor, and comes in white flakes. Anthracene oil is a coal tar fraction, and is available from either oil distributors or chemical suppliers. Mix 90 ounces of naphthalene into 10 ounces of anthracene, and add 20 ounces of this to every 100 gallons of fuel oil. This mixture will help prevent greasy soot deposits that clog burners and reduce efficiency. (Note: Naphthalene is flammable.)

11. *Root Destroyer for Drains*

Into 3 cups caustic soda, mix 1/4 cup copper sulfate and 1 teaspoon ammonium sulfate. Slowly pour 1 cup of this down drain and flush with hot water. (Caution: Handle caustic soda with care. It can cause burns to skin.)

12. *Septic Tank Reactivator*

Into 1 quart water, mix 1 pound brown sugar and 1 envelope dried yeast. Pour this down the toilet and flush so that it will be washed into the tank, where it will promote the anerobic bacteria action that helps the septic tank do its job.

13. *Type Cleaner*

For cleaning not only type, but other parts of your typewriter as well, mix 1 cup water in 1 1/2 cups denatured alcohol. Store this in an airtight container and apply with a rag liberally soaked in this solution. Wipe dry with a clean cloth.

14. *Snow and Ice Melting Compound*

More effective than plain salt, this combination is longer lasting and quicker acting. Mix together 4 cups rock salt, 8 cups ammonium chloride and 4 cups magnesium sulfate. Sprinkle on icy sidewalks or hard-packed snow.

15. *Lighter Fluid*

This is another of the many things that we pay a lot for a little bit of. Especially when it is labeled "Lighter Fluid" and we buy it off the shelf at the drugstore or supermarket. Why not mix your own and store it in a plastic squeeze bottle or something similar? Use 1 pint of deodorized naphtha, add 1/8 teaspoon of citronella oil, and there you are. Be sure to exercise caution and follow the label directions on the naphtha closely. (Note: Deodorized naphtha is flammable.)

$$H-\overset{\overset{\displaystyle H}{|}}{\underset{\underset{\displaystyle H}{|}}{C}}-\mathbf{2}-\overset{\overset{\displaystyle H}{|}}{\underset{\underset{\displaystyle H}{|}}{C}}-H$$

Personal

MAKING SOAP

1. Basic Soap

Making soap is one of those ancient arts that used to be practiced in most homes, and today follows closely upon homemade beer and wine and homemade cheese among the useful skills that many conservation and self-sufficiency-minded people are trying to relearn. The basic art is fairly simple, and once you have done it you may want to experiment by adding ground oatmeal, coconut oil, lemon oil, or whatever strikes your fancy.

First you will need some wooden boxes, or sturdy cardboard ones, for molds. Make them the size you want the cakes to be, 2 inches wide by 2 deep is a good size, and you can make them 20 inches long and cut the bar into four pieces. Then you will need some caustic soda (lye flakes), and a lot of rendered animal fat, or tallow. Use bacon fat, pork fat, or beef fat. Whenever you trim a piece of meat, save the fat in the refrigerator until you have two cups or so and cook it slowly in a pan until the liquid is separated from the fiber. Strain the liquid fat through some cheesecloth and store it in the refrigerator until you have collected six pounds. Now you are ready to make soap.

Put 5 cups cold water in a stainless steel, enamel, or Pyrex bowl. Slowly add 13 ounces caustic soda, stirring with a steel spoon. This mixture will heat up by the chemical action of the lye, and it will eat holes in your clothes and burn your skin if it is splashed about, so be reasonably careful. If you do get some on you, hold the affected area under clear running water for about fifteen minutes. Take the temperature of this lye solution with a glass thermometer and adjust by heating or cooling so that it is 95° F. Meanwhile, melt the 6 pounds tallow over a low fire until it reaches 130° F. and adjust the heat to maintain that temperature. Then pour the lye solution in a thin, even stream into the tallow, stirring constantly until it reaches the consistency of thick syrup. At this point you can add a small amount of perfume, oil of clove, or what you like. Line the mold with an old dishtowel, making sure it is down in the corners, and leave some hanging over the edge. Pour the hot liquid into the mold and cover with the cloth that is hanging over. After twenty-four hours you can take it out of the mold and cut it to size, but it should dry and cure for at least two more weeks. (Note: Caustic soda can cause burns.)

2.   *Heavy-Duty Liquid Hand Soap*

This is a good soap for mechanics' and other very dirty hands. Into 1 cup water mix 2 1/2 teaspoons triethanolamine, and separately mix 5 teaspoons oleic acid into 1 cup kerosene, then stir the kerosene mixture into the water mixture and store in plastic squeeze bottles.

3. *Waterless Hand Soap*

Start by bringing 5 cups water to a boil, turn off the heat, and let cool for a few minutes. Then add 1/2 cup of any powdered white soap, 1/8 cup potassium carbonate, 2 teaspoons trisodium phosphate, and 1/2 cup powdered asbestos. Stir until all are dissolved and let the mixture cool. When it is just warm add a few dashes of lemon oil, and pour into wide-mouth containers. To use, scoop up a teaspoon or so and rub it thoroughly on hands, rinsing with clear water.

HAIR CARE

There are dozens, perhaps hundreds of products sold that are designed for use, one way or another, on hair. Most of them you can make yourself, such as:

1. *Shampoo*

For a concentrated hair shampoo that will go a long way, mix together 1 1/4 cups oleic acid, 1 cup coconut oil, and 1 1/4 cups triethanolamine. A drop or two of an oil base perfume or lemon oil may be added if you wish.

2. *Blond Hair Rinse*

To use as a rinse after shampooing on light-colored hair, this preparation will bring out those glowing highlights! Into 3 3/4 cups water, mix 2 1/2 tablespoons tincture of rhubarb, 1/3 cup isopropyl alcohol and 2 teaspoons propolene glycol. A few drops of your favorite oil base perfume may be added if you wish.

3. Lemon Hair Rinse

Mix 2 tablespoons citric acid and 4 tablespoons tartaric acid into 1 1/2 cups water. Separately put 10 drops lemon oil into 1 cup isopropyl alcohol and then mix the two together. Use this the same as above, as a rinse after shampooing.

4. Hair Set Spray

This keeps hair in place through spring showers; if you want to keep it in place in a hurricane, use less water. Dissolve 1/2 teaspoon acacia and 1 teaspoon borax in 2 cups warm water, then add 6 tablespoons denatured alcohol (type 40) or isopropyl alcohol and a few drops of your favorite perfume, and apply with a plastic spray bottle. (Note: Denatured alcohol is flammable.)

5. Hair Conditioning Cream

We know that longer hair and "the natural look" are in style, but there are times when a little control is necessary: graduation days, big dates, opening nights, when you're going to be photographed at the "Oscar" presentations, or when you just want to look swell in public or private. A small amount of this concoction will let you have fun twice, when you make it and when you use it.

In the top of a double boiler melt 1/4 cup petrolatum, 3/4 tablespoon stearic acid, and 1 teaspoon lanolin. Mix as soon as possible and remove from heat. Then add 1 teaspoon triethanolamine and 1/2 cup water, plus a few drops of an oil base perfume if desired. Use a small amount on fingertips and work into hair thoroughly.

6. *Hair Tonic*

Into 3 cups distilled water mix 4 tablespoons isopropyl alcohol and 1 teaspoon oxyquinoline sulfate. A few drops of a water base perfume may be added as desired. Splash on hands and rub well into hair and scalp.

7. *Hair Wave Lotion*

To help keep that curl in place, dissolve 1/2 teaspoon tragacanth gum in 1/2 cup isopropyl alcohol. Stir in 1 1/2 cups water, 2 teaspoons potassium carbonate, 1/2 teaspoon borax, and a little water base perfume if desired. Dip your comb into this solution to help set hair where you want it.

8. *Wig and Hairpiece Cleaner*

Wigs and other hairpieces have come out of the closet, and are widely accepted, not only as ego boosters, but as fun additions to your costume for special occasions or even for every day. To keep them clean and fresh, mix 1 tablespoon zinc oxide and 2 tablespoons calcium carbonate into 1 cup talc, then add 1 teaspoon boric acid and mix all well. Dust this on the wig or hairpiece, rub it in with the fingers, and brush out thoroughly.

9. *Comb and Hairbrush Cleaner*

This one falls into the category of things grandmother used to do, but it still works better than anything else we have come across. Put roughly 1 tablespoon household ammonia in 2 cups warm water, soak your combs and brushes for about ten minutes, and rinse with clear warm water. (Note: Avoid the vapors of household ammonia.)

MEMOS

BODY THINGS

Here is a collection of things to mix up that will keep you socially acceptable, make you feel good and sometimes look better than you feel.

1. Cucumber Skin Lotion

It has been known for hundreds of years that the juice of that wonderful vegetable the cucumber is not only good taken internally, but has a gentle, cooling, soothing effect when applied to the skin. For a sample, take a good-sized slice and rub it on your face, forehead, the back of your neck. Umm! To make a couple of bottles of the stuff to use any time, first get 4 cups cucumber juice. This may be done by running a few cucumbers through a juicer if you have one, or if not, through a potato ricer. If you use the ricer, strain it through several layers of cheesecloth to remove the pulp. Then, to your 4 cups of juice, add 1 cup glycerin, 1/4 cup isopropyl alcohol and 1 speck benzoic acid. A few drops of rose oil give it a nice smell if you wish.

2. Honey and Almond Lotion

Honey is a remarkable substance. As it comes straight from the hive, it will keep indefinitely, without cooking, without additives, and without refrigeration. People have been using honey in many different ways ever since there were people and bees together on the earth. The ancient Persians, Greeks, and Vikings used it as a food, in a fermented drink known as mead, and in medicines. A honey and almond cream has long been known to be good for the skin. To make your own, you will need two double boilers. In one, put 2 cups water and 2 heaping teaspoons honey. In the other, put 1 1/2 tablespoons stearic acid, 6 tablespoons glycerin, and 2 tablespoons ethylene glycol. Ethylene glycol is permanent antifreeze, available in cans at service stations or auto supply stores. Heat both mixtures to 150° F. and combine them. Allow the mixture to cool to lukewarm and stir in 3 or 4 drops almond oil. Try it out for smell on your wrist, and add a few more drops if you wish.

3.   *Almonds, Lemons, and Limes Cream*

A pleasant and soothing cream may be made with lime water. Soak several slices of a lime in a cup of water overnight, then, to 1 cup lime water, add 1/8 teaspoon glycerin, and stir in 1/8 teaspoon lemon oil, and 1/8 teaspoon almond oil.

4.   *Glycerin Skin Gel*

Glycerin is an emollient, or softening agent, and is excellent for dry skin. Dissolve 5 teaspoons gelatin in 2 1/4 cups hot water, allow it to cool to lukewarm and add 3 tablespoons glycerin. You can also stir in a few drops of any oil base perfume or essential oil, such as rose oil or oil of rosemary.

5.   *Cologne*

This is a pleasant, all-purpose cologne that you can make as given, or alter the proportions to suit your taste. Into 1 cup ethyl alcohol (vodka) mix with constant stirring 40 drops neroli oil, sometimes called orange flower oil, 17 drops lemon oil, 7 drops bergamot oil, and 7 drops rosemary oil.

6.   *All-Purpose Germicidal Cream*

In the top of a double boiler, put 1/2 cup white petrolatum, 3/8 cup mineral oil, and 1/8 cup beeswax, and heat until the wax melts and the ingredients can be stirred together. Separately, put 1 tablespoon borax in 1/4 cup warm water, stirring gently until the borax is dissolved. Then mix these two together and add 1 tablespoon parachlorometacresol. Cool and store in jars.

7. Astringent Lotion

To ease the sting and stop the bleeding from scratches, shaving nicks, and small cuts, mix 1 tablespoon glycerin into 3 cups water, and stir in 2 tablespoons alum. Store in bottles and apply with cotton.

8. Rubbing Alcohol

If you give rubdowns or massages to your high-school or college athletes, your family, friends, or lovers, make 2 cups of denatured alcohol (type 40) or isopropyl alcohol more suited to the task by adding 1/2 teaspoon glycerin and 1/2 teaspoon castor oil.

9. Stiff Muscle Rub

Same as above, but this is for more severe cases, such as when you decide that you really should take up tennis again, or jogging, and suffer the consequences of having been desk- and automobile-bound all those years. Into 1 1/2 cups denatured alcohol (type 40) or isopropyl alcohol, mix 1/2 cup methyl salicylate, 1/8 teaspoon camphor, and 1/8 teaspoon menthol. When these are well mixed, stir in 1/4 cup mineral oil. Use for rubdowns, applying just enough pressure with fingers and heel of the hand to make your victim wince, but not actually scream in pain.

10. Antiperspirant Liquid

It has struck us as rather amusing that several commercial manufacturers have come out with an "unscented" version of their antiperspirants. If you're tired of spending all that money for those aerosol cans, which, by the way, are becoming an increasingly serious source of both air and solid waste pollution, it's easy to make your own. Mix 1/2 cup denatured alcohol (type 40) or isopropyl alcohol into 2 1/2 cups water, and thoroughly stir in one tablespoon powdered alum, and 1 tablespoon powdered zinc oxide. A plastic squeeze bottle that can be reused is perfect for this. Shake before using.

11. Deodorant Cream

If you prefer the cream variety, that's easy too. Heat 2 cups water and 1/4 cup stearic acid until the stearic acid is dissolved. Separately mix 2 tablespoons triethanolamine in 1 1/2 cups water, and add that to the first mixture. Cool to lukewarm and stir in 2 tablespoons powdered alum, and pour immediately into jars.

12. Deodorant Powder

On the other hand, if you prefer a powder that you can sprinkle around in your shoes, on the dog, and other odd places, simply mix together 1/3 cup talc, 1/4 cup boric acid, and 1 tablespoon powdered alum. A few drops of a non—oil base perfume will give it your favorite smell. You can use an old baby powder container or make a shaker can out of almost anything that has a lid you can make small holes in. A large salt shaker works fine.

13. Baby Oil

Many products are advertised in such a way that they hit us in our conscience. Are we doing right by our child? Our health? Nine out of ten doctors recommend blank, so why aren't *you* buying it? The trick is to get you to pay a lot for something you don't really need. Take baby oil. Buy the U.S.P. grade white mineral oil—about a pint is a good quantity—add a few drops of an oil base perfume if you wish, and there you are. As with the higher priced stuff, a little goes a long way, so apply sparingly to baby's bottom.

14. Bubble Bath

Bubble baths are fun for kids and adults alike, but kids seem to enjoy them especially. In fact they are often the only way kids will take a bath without a fight. If you have more than one or two kids, keeping them supplied with appropriate bubble baths can take a surprising bite out of the budget, so you might enjoy mixing your own for fun and profit.

Take 3 cups sodium sesquicarbonate, 1 3/4 cups sodium lauryl sulfate, and 1 teaspoon sodium alginate. Stir together and add a few drops of water base perfume if you wish. Use a couple of tablespoons of this under running water in the tub.

15. Suntan Lotion

For that tan that people will notice and that will also save you money, mix 5 tablespoons isopropyl alcohol and 2 tablespoons glycerin into 2 cups water. Add a little food coloring and water base perfume if you desire.

16. Burn Treatment

For skin burns, our mothers and grandmothers used to tell us to put some butter or lard on it and wrap it up to keep it clean. In this case mother didn't know best. The latest medical information on burns makes good sense if you think about it. The skin and adjacent tissue has been damaged by heat, so what you should do is cool the area down. This is best accomplished by soaking the area that has been burned in cool water for prolonged periods of time, which means an hour or two. Don't wrap it in gauze or bandages, keep it soaking in cool water. If the burn is serious or extensive, seek medical treatment.

17. Petroleum Jelly

For a Vaseline-type jelly with all sorts of uses, from lubricating to removing paint and plaster from skin, melt 1/2 cup white petrolatum and 3 tablespoons paraffin wax in the top of a double boiler. Remove from heat and allow to cool till just warm, then pour in 2 cups mineral oil, stirring thoroughly. Pour in jars or other containers and cool to room temperature.

HANDS AND FACE

The hands come first with:

1. *Lotion for Chapped Hands*

Into 1/3 cup denatured alcohol (type 40) or isopropyl alcohol, mix 2/3 cup glycerin and 2 tablespoons peanut oil. Stir well, then add 1 teaspoon powdered tragacanth and 2 teaspoons tincture of benzoin.

2. *Cream for Chapped Lips*

Melt 1/4 cup beeswax in the top of a double boiler; when it has melted, remove from the fire and stir in 1/4 cup castor oil, 3 tablespoons sesame oil and 2 tablespoons anhydrous lanolin. Pour into small jars and allow to cool. To use, rub a finger in the jar and apply a small amount to the lips.

3. *Cooling Hand Lotion*

Into 3/4 cup water, mix 1 1/2 cups denatured alcohol (type 40) or isopropyl alcohol, 1/4 cup glycerin, and 1/8 teaspoon menthol crystals. Again, a few drops of a non–oil base perfume may be added if you like.

4. Fingernail Hardener

Fingernails contain no calcium, in contrast to bones and other parts of the body, so it is difficult to see how calcium tablets help strengthen them, although some people claim that they do. If you have trouble keeping your nails from splitting or tearing, or if, for example, you play the guitar and need a good strong set of right-hand nails, mix up 3 tablespoons water, 1 tablespoon glycerin, and 1 teaspoon powdered alum. Coat your nails with the solution at night using a small brush, or by dipping. In the morning remove with denatured alcohol (type 40) or isopropyl alcohol and a piece of cotton.

5. Fingernail Softener

If, on the other hand, your nails are so hard and dry that they crack and chip and you want to soften them up, paint them with a mixture of 3 tablespoons triethanolamine in 1/2 cup water, to which you slowly stir in 2 tablespoons of either castor or olive oil. This can be washed off in the morning with water.

6. Wrinkle Lotion for Skin

This is to help tighten and smooth the places where all of us will eventually have wrinkles. Into 1 quart distilled water, mix 2 teaspoons tincture of benzoin, 2 teaspoons glycerin, 1/4 teaspoon alum, and 1 speck of zinc sulfate. A few drops of your favorite non–oil base perfume may be added to suit you. Shake thoroughly to mix all ingredients, run it through a filter paper to remove any undissolved particles, and store in a bottle.

7. Beauty Mask

If you've ever gone to a beauty parlor and spent ten or twenty dollars or more for one of these, you will know how great they feel. Well, pamper yourself, not the cash box at the beauty parlor! Mix together 4 cups powdered clay, 1 cup talc, and 1/8 cup titanium dioxide. Add water a little at a time, stirring it around until it reaches the consistency of thick paint. Then, with a soft brush such as a large camel's hair watercolor brush, paint your face with it, let it dry, and after about thirty minutes wash it off with water.

8. *Refreshing Face Wash*

To 3/4 cup denatured alcohol (type 40) or isopropyl alcohol, add 6 tablespoons witch hazel, 4 tablespoons glycerin, and a few drops of a non—oil base perfume.

9. *Cold Cream*

This is virtually the same as any commercial cold cream; use it to remove makeup and for general skin cleaning and conditioning. Put 2 cups mineral oil and 1/2 cup white beeswax into the top of a double boiler and heat until the beeswax is melted, then allow it to cool down to 120° F. In a separate pan put 1 cup water and heat that to 120° F. Add 1 1/2 tablespoons powdered borax to the water and stir gently until it is dissolved. Then, very slowly, stirring all the while, pour the water and borax mixture into the oil and wax mixture. Cool until it just starts to solidify, and pour into containers.

10. *Allover Skin Cream*

For a cream that you can use wherever you want to, on dry spots such as ankles, knees, and elbows, or whatnot, heat 1 cup white petrolatum and 3/4 tablespoon anhydrous lanolin in a double boiler. In a separate pan warm 2 cups water to which has been added 1 teaspoon glycerin. When both mixtures are warm, stir them together, cool until it just starts to solidify and add a few drops of a non—oil base perfume or essence if you wish.

11. Skin Softener

To soften and moisten places that have seen hard wear or that perhaps you have neglected, this is a heavy-duty moistening agent. Mix 3/4 cup white mineral oil and 1/4 cup olive oil. To this you may add just a few drops of an oil base perfume or essence.

12. Body and Face Powder

Again this is something that is remarkably inexpensive until it gets put into those beautiful containers that you see at the beauty bar in the department stores. In a bowl put 2 cups talc, 2 tablespoons boric acid, and 1/2 cup cornstarch and mix with a fork. You may use it as is, or at this point, if you want to give it a little color and smell, add a few drops of a non–oil base dye or coloring and keep stirring until it is thoroughly mixed in and you have achieved the color you want. Start with red and experiment with small amounts of orange or yellow. The same for the perfume. Note: Food coloring is fine for this.

13. After-Shave Lotion

Into 1 cup water mix 1/4 cup denatured alcohol (type 40) or isopropyl alcohol and 5 tablespoons glycerin. Then add 1/4 cup witch hazel, 1/2 teaspoon powdered alum, 1/4 teaspoon boric acid, and a few drops of a non–oil base perfume, however much suits your taste.

14. Electric After-Shave Lotion

For an after-shave lotion that is simultaneously bracing and soothing, mix 1 cup water, 1/4 cup witch hazel, 1/4 cup denatured alcohol, 5 tablespoons glycerin, 1/2 teaspoon powdered alum, 1/4 teaspoon boric acid and a water base perfume to suit your taste. Splash it on liberally and enjoy the fruits of your own labors.

15. Electric Pre-Shave Lotion

For a pre-shave lotion to smooth your skin and stiffen the beard, mix 2 tablespoons glycerin and 3/4 cup water into 1 cup isopropyl alcohol. Add a few drops of a water base perfume if you desire, and store in a container with a good seal on the top.

16. Cosmetic Remover

This is easier to make than the cleansing cream, so you might want to try it first and see how you like it. If it doesn't suit you, then try the cleansing cream. In the top of a double boiler melt 1/2 cup yellow beeswax and 1/3 cup paraffin wax. When they are melted and can be stirred together, remove from heat and stir in 1 cup mineral oil. Cool and pour into jars. Wipe it on with a cotton swab or a tissue and wipe off with a dry tissue.

17. Acne Lotion

When the skin becomes extrasensitive to irritation and infection, regular washing with the following solution will help to keep it dry and clean.

To 1/2 cup of distilled water add 4 tablespoons isopropyl alcohol and 1 1/2 teaspoons glycerin. Then stir in 1/8 teaspoon triethanolamine and a few drops of water base perfume if you wish. First wash with soap and water, then wipe skin with a piece of cotton soaked in this lotion.

18. Liquid Mascara

For highlighting eyelashes and eyebrows, mix 10 drops of an oil base black dye into 4 tablespoons tincture of benzoin. Keep it in any small container with a screw-on cap, and apply with a soft brush.

The Formula Book
MEMOS

TEETH

Along with nearly everything else, toothpaste, of all things, has gone up in price rather dramatically. So in the spirit of economy, here are some things you can have fun making, while you save money and take care of your teeth, whether they are your own or they came from the tooth factory.

1. Toothpaste

Take 1/2 cup powdered pumice, and add to it 1/4 cup glycerin, stirring as you do to form a paste. Add a few drops of oil of peppermint for flavor, and use by dipping the dry bristles of your toothbrush into the jar, or whatever you keep it in.

2. Denture Adhesive

Into 1/2 cup powdered tragacanth mix 2 tablespoons powdered acacia and 1 1/2 teaspoons boric acid. Sprinkle a small amount of this on a wet dental plate.

3. Foaming Denture Cleaner

Take one cup warm water and stir in 1 tablespoon sodium perborate. Drop your plate into the cup for a few minutes, and then rinse.

4. Nonfoaming Denture Cleaner

For a change of pace, into 1 cup isopropyl alcohol stir 1 teaspoon citric acid and 10 drops peppermint oil. Soak your dentures in this and rinse off under clear water.

5.   *Swedish Formula Mouthwash*

From the land of superb engineering, sensational movie actresses, a rather militant neutrality, and one of the highest standards of living in the world, a mouthwash? Yes, a mouthwash. Into 4 cups water, mix 1/16 teaspoon borax (measure this by taking a level quarter-teaspoonful and estimating 1/4 of that), 1 1/2 teaspoons boric acid, and, if you wish, a few drops of essence of cloves and perhaps some red food coloring.

6.   *An American Mouthwash*

After that brief excursion we are back home again. This one's not as simple, but it has that zing that we are used to. Into 1/2 cup denatured alcohol (type 37) mix 1 speck menthol crystals and a few drops cinnamon oil. Add the result to 4 cups water, and then stir in 2 tablespoons sodium bicarbonate, 1 tablespoon borax, 1/8 teaspoon zinc chloride (again, measure this by taking a level quarter-teaspoonful and estimating half), 1 cup glycerin, and, if you wish, some red food coloring.

EYES

If you live in or near any large city in this country you face, from time to time, an irritating level of air pollution that gets you right in the eyes. There are now some local laws which prohibit smoking in public places such as elevators and public rooms of certain kinds, but until such laws are more widespread and more effective we all need to protect our eyes.

1.   *Soothing Eyewash*

To ease the sting on those days when you can't see across town, thoroughly dissolve 1/16 teaspoon sodium bicarbonate in 1 cup distilled water. (Measure 1/4 teaspoonful and estimate a quarter of that to get 1/16 teaspoon.) Use an eye dropper or an eyewash cup to rinse the surface of your eyes.

2. Contact Lens Fluid

Again, instead of buying some mysterious and probably magical (because it's so expensive) fluid, you can make your own in five minutes and for less than a penny. Into 1/2 cup distilled water, mix 1/8 teaspoon bicarbonate of soda and 1/8 teaspoon salt. Stir until the soda and the salt are dissolved and put in a small bottle with a dropper to dispense into your contact lens storage case. You may want to run the solution through a paper coffee filter to make sure there are no particles of undissolved salt or soda in the liquid.

FEET

Our feet are probably the most neglected part of our anatomy. As they are farthest away from the rest of us, this may be understandable, but we stand around on them, walk and run on them all day, and what do they get for this punishment which they endure in an attitude of silent patience and devotion to duty? Probably no more than a cursory wipe with a soapy washcloth at the end of the day and that only after all the other parts of our body have been served first. Feet, in our estimation, deserve more kindly attention, for where would we be without them?

1. Soothing Foot Bath

A special bath, where they can relax and soak in the nice hot water and perhaps receive a bit of a massage, is a welcome reward. Mix together 1/8 teaspoon menthol crystals, 4 tablespoons powdered alum, 8 tablespoons boric acid, and 10 tablespoons magnesium sulfate (Epsom salts). Use a teaspoon of this in a gallon of hot water.

2. Athlete's Foot Powder

If you have been so negligent as to let your feet get in this condition, shame! However, here is the remedy. Into 1 cup powdered boric acid, mix 2/3 cup talc and 1/3 cup powdered sodium thiosulfate. Sprinkle on feet, being sure to get it in between the toes where it can do some good.

$$H-\underset{\underset{\displaystyle H}{|}}{\overset{\overset{\displaystyle H}{|}}{C}}-3-\underset{\underset{\displaystyle H}{|}}{\overset{\overset{\displaystyle H}{|}}{C}}-H$$

Automotive and Mechanical

Most of us who own cars spend some money, time, and effort keeping them clean and presentable: the traditional Sunday afternoon with a cold lemonade, beer, or gin and tonic, the hose, sponges, wax, and polishing cloths, keeping the buggy in shape. Others, except for those fortunate few who know an honest and reasonable mechanic, have been shocked at the bills presented by the garage and have been inspired by fear and inflation to learn a bit about the technical aspects. Once you find that a forty dollar tune-up can be done for fifteen dollars or less and a few hours or less of your time, it is suddenly not such a mysterious thing and is easy to learn how to do after all. To go along with this trend, here are a few suggestions for things you can make that will help you with the finish, with the engine and related parts, and with cleaning it all up.

TAKING CARE OF THE OUTSIDE

1. Car Soap

Ordinary soap generally won't touch the road grease, squashed insects, and other assorted flying objects that stick to the outside of your car, so here is a soap that will. Dissolve 3 tablespoons caustic potash flakes in 1 cup water. In a slow stream, stir this into 2 cups corn oil, and add a little more water if necessary to obtain a liquid consistency. Use about two tablespoons in a bucket of water. (Caution: Handle the caustic potash with care. It can cause burns.)

2. Car Liquid Wax

To protect the finish from sun and storm, and make it easier to keep clean, you should keep it waxed—probably once every three months or so is sufficient, depending on the climate you live in. In a double boiler heat 1/2 cup ceresin wax and 2 tablespoons yellow beeswax until they melt. Stir and allow to cool until the mixture just starts to solidify; then slowly stir in 2 cups turpentine and 1 tablespoon pine oil. Apply with a piece of old towel, or something similar, and polish with a clean soft cloth. As with most waxes, so with this one and the next; it's best to do a section at a time, such as one door, polish it, then the next, and so on. This is to prevent the wax film from drying too hard so that it is difficult to polish. It will dry initially in a few minutes, but it keeps on getting harder for the next hour or two. (Note: Turpentine is flammable.)

3. Car Paste Wax

The same remarks we made about floor waxes apply here. If you prefer the harder, longer lasting finish of a paste wax, try this one. In a double boiler again, melt 2 tablespoons yellow beeswax,

5 tablespoons ceresin wax, 9 tablespoons carnauba wax, and 3 tablespoons montan wax. Remove from heat, allow to cool a little, and stir in 2 cups mineral oil, 4 tablespoons turpentine, and 1 tablespoon pine oil. Allow to cool a little more, pour into cans, and cool to room temperature. (Note: Turpentine is flammable.)

4.   Polishing Cloth

Similar cloths are sold under several different trade names, and they are usually referred to as "magic" or by some other superlative, but they are all basically the same as this one. Into 1 cup water mix 1 tablespoon silicone water emulsion. Take a clean flannel cloth (one-foot square is a convenient size), and soak it well in this mixture. Wring out gently and let dry. Wiping the car with this does two things: it picks up dust and leaves a very thin film of silicone, which gives a very nice shine. Shake out the cloth to get rid of the dust and it can be used over and over again. When it becomes too dirty, either wash it out and give it the silicone treatment again, or, if it is too far gone, discard it and make a new one.

Incidentally, many record cleaning cloths are treated in the same way. If you have fine records that you care about, these cloths should not be used, as they deposit a film which, after many applications, can build up in the grooves and cause trouble. The best thing to use on records is very fine pile nylon velvet. If you have trouble with static electricity attracting dust onto the record surface, dampen the cloth ever so slightly with distilled water. It must not be so damp that it transfers any moisture to the record, just damp enough to get rid of the static charge. Do not use it with silicone emulsion or anything else that will leave a film on the record. The fine nylon pile will get down in the grooves to pick up dust, and this is usually enough.

5.   Windshield Cleaning and De-Icing

For those who live in areas with severe winters and who must drive in all weathers, this is an excellent preparation to put in the windshield washer reservoir. Also carry a bottle in the glove compartment or trunk; sometimes the rear and side windows can ice up and ruin your visibility. Dissolve 1 ounce granulated soap into 20 ounces water, and add this to 1/2 gallon ethylene glycol, mix in 3/4 ounce gelatin, 1/2 ounce gum tragacanth, and 9 ounces mineral oil.

6. Antifog Preparation

To prevent the inside from fogging up, mix 1 tablespoon silicone liquid emulsion into 3 cups water, dampen a soft cloth and rub over the insides of all the windows.

TAKING CARE OF THE INSIDE

A friend of ours has a slogan, "Prevent Junkyards, Drive a Wreck." He derives a good deal of satisfaction from keeping his "wreck" in remarkably good running condition, and it repays him by going thirty miles for every gallon of gasoline he feeds it. So, for the weekend putterers and the growing number of amateur mechanics, here is a handful of odds and ends to help keep our wrecks together.

1. Radiator Leak Sealer

Into 7/8 cup water mix 1 cup sulfite liquor and 1/8 cup powdered asbestos. Pour about a pint of this into the radiator, fill with water, and run the engine for about fifteen minutes. (Caution: Do not inhale dust of asbestos powder.)

2. Radiator Cleaner

Ideally, the water, or whatever you run in the radiator to cool the engine, should be clean and clear. If it is murky and full of sludge, clean it out with washing soda as follows. (If the water is full of rust particles, see number 3 below.) Into 3 quarts warm water mix 2 1/2 cups washing soda. Drain the radiator and add this mixture, fill to the top with water, and run the engine for half an hour. Then drain and flush out the radiator with clear water until it runs clear out of the drain plug.

3.   Radiator Rust Remover

As noted above, if the radiator water is rusty use this instead of number 2. Into 2 gallons water mix 4 ounces oxalic acid and 4 ounces sodium bisulfite. Drain the radiator and fill it with this, run the engine for one hour, drain and flush with clear water, then refill it with water or antifreeze. (Caution: Oxalic acid is toxic. Do not take it internally, breathe its vapors, or allow contact with skin.)

4.   Radiator Scale Remover

If you live in an area with very hard water, the coolant may be clean, but the radiator can lose efficiency and become clogged by the formation of scale, or mineral deposits from the water. If this is a problem, the scale can be seen by removing the radiator cap and looking down inside. If it looks like the inside of an old teakettle, mix 6 ounces of trisodium phosphate in 4 gallons water. Drain the radiator and fill it with this mixture. Run the engine slowly, a little above idle speed, for about twenty minutes. Drain, flush, and refill with clean water or antifreeze.

5.   Radiator Scale Preventer

If you have solved the problem we just discussed in number 4 above, but are still using hard water, you can prevent the recurrence of scale buildup by mixing 3 ounces sodium silicate and 1 ounce trisodium phosphate in a gallon of water and filling your radiator with that.

6.   Radiator Rust Preventer

Again, if you have solved the problem of rust by using number 3 above, you will want to prevent more rust from eating away the insides of your cooling system. For each gallon of water that your radiator holds, mix in 6 tablespoons dimethylmorpholine. This is a flammable liquid, so use caution in handling it.

7.   Antifreeze

To make an antifreeze solution, you need nothing more than some liquid which will mix with water, which has a lower freezing point than water, and which will not vaporize at high temperatures. This last requirement rules out alcohol, a common antifreeze agent where high temperatures are not encountered, but ethylene glycol fills the bill, and that is what is used in most automobile antifreeze preparations. To mix your own, use the following guidelines: Where the lowest overnight temperature is 0° F., mix 4 pints ethylene glycol to one gallon water. For -10° F., use 5 pints per gallon; for -20° F., use 8 pints per gallon.

8.   Leak Seal for Tires

If you have tubeless tires, which nearly everyone does these days, and one or more of them has a slow leak but enough tread left that you don't want to replace it, use this sealer. The liquid latex emulsion can often be found in good hobby shops, and the sodium silicate is our old friend, waterglass. Mix 1/2 cup sodium silicate with 1 cup liquid latex emulsion. If the tire is on the car, jack up the car just enough to take the weight off the tire. Deflate the tire by removing the valve, and pour 1/4 cup into the tire casing using a small funnel. Clean the inside of the valve housing, replace the valve, and reinflate the tire.

9. Gasoline Antiknock Additive

Here's a real money saver. If your chariot won't go on regular gas and the super is eating up your pocketbook, mix up 1 cup denatured alcohol (any type), 1/2 cup benzene, and 1 tablespoon hydrogen peroxide. Add just 1 teaspoon to the tank for every five gallons of gasoline. (Note: Denatured alcohol and benzene are flammable. Avoid contact of hydrogen peroxide with eyes and skin.)

10. Gasoline Engine Cleaning Additive

This is a simply made additive which will keep new and recently overhauled engines clean and break up carbon deposits that form in combustion chambers around valves and spark plugs and cause a loss of efficiency. Melt 1 cup paraffin in the top of a double boiler and stir in 1 cup of SAE 30 motor oil. Allow this to cool to room temperature and use 5 ounces in the tank for each five gallons of gasoline. Usually running one tankful of this every few months is sufficient.

11. Battery Terminal Protective Coating

All battery terminals will corrode in time, and if it gets really bad, corrosion can shorten the life of the battery. We recently had to purchase a new battery, and would like to report that it is not just the cost of oil that is going out of sight. In any case, it has always been true that a little preventive maintenance pays off handsomely in the long run. This is another simple preparation that really works. Mix together 1 cup sodium silicate and 1 cup water, and paint this on the terminals and the cable connections. If there is some corrosion present, it should be cleaned off with a wire brush first.

12. *Lubricating Oil*

This is an excellent penetrating oil to spray into hard-to-reach places to stop squeaks and keep doors, springs, and so on operating smoothly. Mix 3 ounces rape seed oil into 1 quart paraffin oil. Use in a pump-type oil can or plastic squeeze bottle.

CLEANING UP

Even if you have never done any mechanical work on your car, it is obvious from looking at gas station attendants that if you do you are going to get pretty dirty. An equally obvious way of keeping the grime to a minimum is to have a reasonably clean engine to work on and to keep your tools clean and in good condition. We have found that taking the time for both of these, without being fanatic about it, can reduce frustration and make the job go more smoothly. Although there are some people who can tell the difference between 1/2" and 9/16" just by looking, it helps to be able to see the size markings on your wrenches, which you can't do if they are covered with black grease. So have a good supply of recycleable rags, and wipe your tools and hands from time to time, giving the tools an extra good cleaning before putting them away.

1. *Engine and Parts Degreasing Compound*

Mix together 3 1/2 cups trisodium phosphate, 1 cup bicarbonate of soda and 1/2 cup sodium metasilicate. Depending on how big the job is, put 1/2 cup or so of this in an old coffee can or similar container, mix in enough water to form a thin paste and brush it on the parts to be cleaned, being sure to get it in all the cracks and crannies. Let it stand for about fifteen minutes and wash it off with a brush and clear water. If what you're working on is heavily encrusted with hard, black, gritty grease, it will doubtless need another application and a little elbow grease.

90

2. Tool Rust Remover

One should not allow tools to become rusty, of course, but if you have inherited someone else's neglect, a mixture of 1 tablespoon ammonium citrate crystals in 2 cups water will clean up rusty tools if you soak them in it overnight. Wipe them clean with a rag, and apply a light coat of oil to protect them.

3. Antirust Tool Coating

If some of your tools are particularly susceptible to rust, or if you are going to store them away for the winter, this preparation will keep them pristine and does not have to be removed before you use them. Melt 1 cup lanolin in a double boiler and stir in 1 cup petrolatum (petroleum jelly). While still warm, brush a thin coat on tools, shovels, rakes, and so on. If the object is small enough it can be dipped.

4. Garage Floor Cleaner

In chapter 1 we gave you a concrete floor cleaner good for heavy-duty cleaning. If you just want to clean up oil spills and minor crud, use this simpler version. Into 3 cups powdered soap, mix 6 tablespoons sodium metasilicate. Use 1 cup of this mixture in a gallon of warm water.

$$\underset{H}{\overset{H}{\vphantom{|}}}H-\underset{H}{\overset{H}{C}}-\mathbf{4}-\underset{H}{\overset{H}{C}}-H$$

Garden, Agricultural, and Livestock

If you're not a weekend mechanic, chances are you are a weekend gardener. More and more people are taking their cue from Candide and cultivating their own gardens. Gardening is good for fun, flowers, and a bit of food, not to mention possible profit, emotional as well as monetary. While most people restrict themselves to vegetable growing, an increasing number are finding that you don't have to live in the country to have a livestock population. 4-H youngsters have known for a long time that a rabbit hutch or small chicken coop in a suburban backyard can be fun and educational and can provide fresh meat for the table at the same time. An additional benefit is that the manure from such an operation is excellent fertilizer for vegetables. Many of us live such insulated, prepackaged lives that we shrink from the thought of the necessary steps to get the chicken from the coop to the kitchen, but surely for many of our mothers and probably most of our grandmothers, part of the week's routine was to cheerfully wring the neck of the bird that was to grace the

Sunday dinner table. One naturally thinks that if Granny knew how to do it, what's wrong with us? We have read some place that a chicken who is fed a teaspoon of whiskey before he is killed dies happier and the meat is tenderer. Perhaps a little nip for the executioner as well as the victim will make the whole operation relatively painless.

Some of what follows is obviously for those who *do* live in the country, but much of it can be used by the backyard gardener as well.

CARING FOR YOUR PLANTS AND GARDEN

1. *Fertilizer for Azaleas*

These are such beautiful and popular flowering bushes that it is easy to get into growing them in more than a casual manner. In fact one of our acquaintances has a considerable side-business in them which started purely from the love of flowers and grew into an amazing income-producing venture. For this fertilizer, get a bushel basket of sawdust, and thoroughly stir into it 9 cups potash, 1 1/2 cups superphosphate, and 1 1/3 cups ammonium sulfate. Mix this with equal parts of earth, plant your azaleas, and stand back.

2. *Fertilizer for House Plants*

Some house plants such as African violets need special care, but a good general fertilizer for your average dieffenbachia or philodendron is a mixture of 3 ounces sodium phosphate and 4 ounces potassium nitrate. Mix 1 tablespoon to a gallon of water. Feeding this once every two weeks should keep your plants happy if they have good light; feed them a little less often if the light is poor. For plants that need special care, consult your local nursery. Maintaining friendly thoughts and a happy atmosphere may help as well. It certainly won't hurt your plants, or you either for that matter.

93

3. Wound Dressing for Trees and Shrubs

Just as with a person, if one of your trees gets into an altercation with a car or truck, it is a good idea to dress the wounds to prevent infection or infestation by parasites. We hope you don't place your trees and shrubs in such precarious positions, however, and probably the most common source of wounds for them is from your pruning shears or saw. Pruning is essential for healthy growth in many varieties, and the pruning of old or weak branches leaves a scar that is much easier to heal and much less susceptible to infestation by parasites than is the ragged break of a branch that gets torn off in a wind.

Mix together 1 cup zinc oxide and 2 cups mineral oil and apply a good coating with a brush to stubs of trimmed branches or any areas where the bark has been extensively damaged and scraped or cut off down to the sapwood.

4. Whitewash

For your Tom Sawyer chores it's quite easy to make the whitewash. The tricky part is getting someone else to wield the brush. Into 1 gallon water, mix 2 pounds salt, and slowly stir in 7 pounds hydrated lime. Then look around for an unsuspecting young child, and go into your speech about the virtues of painting fences. (Caution: Hydrated lime is caustic and can cause burns.)

5. Fence Post Preservative

Before you whitewash the fence, you have to have a fence. And if you want to have the fence around for a while, and the posts are to be of wood, they should be treated with a preservative so that the below-ground portions will be protected from dry rot, termites, and other corrupting influences. Into 1 gallon water mix 1 3/4 pounds zinc chloride until it is dissolved. Stand the posts in a large can such as a garbage can, and fill with this solution two or three inches above the depth the posts will be in

94

the ground. For example, if the post holes are to be a foot and a half deep, the solution should be twenty or twenty-one inches deep. Let them soak for a full twenty-four hours, and then let them dry. If you have ever dug post holes by hand with a post hole digger, you will know that it is not an easy job. If you have a hundred feet or more of fence to put in, it will probably take a couple of days to dig the holes unless you have lots of help, so there is plenty of time to let the posts soak in this preservative.

6. *Composting*

With the increasing popularity of backyard gardening, more people are becoming conservation conscious, recycling cans and bottles, as well as vegetable waste matter. Instead of burning up leaves and grass clippings and putting vegetable trimmings out with the garbage, you can put them into a compost pile where they decompose and can then be returned to the soil with great profit. There are many methods of composting, but the best we have tried is the above-ground method. Use a fairly open fence, such as snow fencing, and make an enclosure about 3 feet by 6 feet, or larger, depending on the size of your garden and the amount of waste vegetable matter you have available for composting. The open, above-ground pile allows air to circulate through it, and speeds up the decay process while preventing the stuff from putrifying. Alternate layers a few inches thick of vegetable trimmings and soil. Along with the vegetable trimmings, grass clippings, and leaves, you can add old newspapers; they decay very nicely. The layer of soil can also contain some manure if you have a horse or some chickens or rabbits. Do not use bones or meat scraps, bones will not decay and the meat scraps will only turn putrid and cause very bad odors, attracting dogs and generally causing more problems than you need. Keep the pile moist but not wet, and in about six or eight weeks turn it over. The best way to do this is to have an identical enclosure next to the one your pile is in, and take off the top layers with a shovel or pitch fork, putting them on the bottom of the neighboring bin upside down. In about six more weeks you should have good compost, ready to spade into the garden soil.

The Formula Book

MEMOS

96

GETTING RID OF PESTS

Depending on the part of the country you live in, you will have a specialized set of control problems. In fact, the specific location, your special valley or hill, can have plant parasites and other disease-causing organisms that, amazingly enough, are found perhaps nowhere else on earth. For these special problems your state university agricultural extension service is probably the best source of advice. There are some universal aggravations, however, and we here offer you some reasonable antidotes for a few of them.

1. *Grass Killer*

A nice green lawn is what most people try to achieve, not to get rid of; but there are places where grass can be a problem. Grass of the Bermuda type, which sends out long runners, can encroach on areas where it is not wanted, such as driveways and patios, and grass and weeds can go wild in untended back portions of the lot near the alleyway. Attempting to dig it out has two disadvantages: it's a lot of work, and it is impossible to get out all the roots, so in a month or less it grows back. A simple mixture of 1 pound of calcium chloride in 1 gallon water sprinkled on superfluous grass will kill it, making removal much easier, or you can just let it lie there and rot, enriching the soil, which can later be put to some more useful purpose.

2. *Dandelion Plant and Root Killer*

A friend of ours once said that if dandelions weren't considered a weed, people would grow them. They are useful; the tender young leaves can be eaten in salads, and the flowers are used in some homemade wines. But if you are trying to get them out of the lawn, they can be very tenacious. We give two methods for eliminating them, the first for larger, heavily infested areas,

97

the second for smaller lawns and few enough plants so that they can be treated individually.

Into 1 gallon kerosene mix 1 pint denatured alcohol (any type) and 1 pound bran oil, and spray this over the area with an agricultural sprayer. The bran oil is also known as furfural-dehyde, and is a toxic agent that can be absorbed through the skin, so be sure to read and follow all label precautions.

If you can treat individual plants, here is a direct and less toxic method. Into 1 gallon kerosene mix 1 cup paraffin oil. Cut the root an inch or two below the ground with a dandelion root cutter, which you can either make or buy at the local garden store. It's long and narrow with a sharp V at the end. Pull out the plant and squirt in a shot of the mixture with a pump oil can, plastic squeeze bottle, or other suitable container. You can cut the root below ground by putting the cutter into the ground an inch or two away from the plant, angled downward about thirty degrees and aiming directly for the stem; the roots generally grow straight down for quite a distance.

3. Algae Spray for Ponds

If you are lucky enough to live in the country and have a pond, you may be unlucky enough to be troubled with the green slimy scum of an algal bloom from time to time, especially in warmer weather. Use 5 gallons water into which you have mixed 1 gallon sodium pentachlorophenate, and spray this on the surface of the pond at the rate of at most 1 gallon per 1,000 square feet.

4. Ant Mound Eradicator

To 2 gallons water, add 1/4 cup of any liquid soap or dish-washing detergent, and 1 teaspoon pyrethrin. Pour one cup on each ant mound, and repeat after an hour to make sure that the mixture penetrates down into all the galleries and tunnels of the ant colony.

5. *Carpenter Ant Exterminator*

Into 2 quarts kerosene mix 2 cups paradichlorobenzene or moth crystals until they are dissolved. This solution should then be sprayed on bushes or other areas where the ants are present.

6. *Japanese Beetle Spray for Trees and Bushes*

These destructive insects have been brought fairly well under control, but there are still occasional problems with them in various parts of the country. To 10 gallons water add 2 pounds hydrated lime and 5 ounces alum, stirring until dissolved. Apply this with an agricultural sprayer, making sure that the undersides of the leaves are coated as well as the tops. (Caution: Hydrated lime is caustic and can cause burns.)

7. *Garden Insecticide*

Pyrethrin is made from chrysanthemums, is used in many different insecticides, and is mildly toxic if taken internally. But handled properly it is one of the best and least toxic to animals of all the chemical insecticides used. For a solution that will discourage most garden pests, mix 1 cup pyrethrin in 2 quarts kerosene, and add 2 quarts water and 1/4 cup liquid soap or dishwashing detergent. The kerosene may damage some delicate plants, so it is a good idea to ask your local nurseryman or test it in a small area if you have any doubts.

8. *Rabbit Repellent*

Dissolve 1 cup gum rosin into 1 quart denatured alcohol (any type). Spray or paint around the base of trees, shrubs, fence posts, and so on.

FOR THE ANIMALS

If you assume ownership of an animal, whether it's a pet, a working animal or livestock, you also assume responsibility for its health and general comfort. No one wants to be burdened with a sick animal, so, just as you take preventive measures to maintain your own health, you can take preventive measures to maintain the health of your animals. Besides regular checkups by a veterinarian and the appropriate vaccinations and inoculations, it's important to keep their living and eating areas clean and to keep them as free as possible of fleas, ticks, and other bothersome pests.

1.   Flea Soap

Into 5 cups kerosene mix 1/2 cup oleic acid, and then add 1/4 cup triethanolamine. Use this as soap, with water, to wash the dogs or other animals that are bothered by fleas. Rub it in well and let it stand for ten minutes before rinsing off. This can also be used as a spray to control fleas in kennels and sleeping areas by mixing it with equal parts of water.

2.   Insect Repellent for Animals.

There are reasons other than comfort for keeping your animals from being driven to distraction by flies and gnats. Flies, of course, can cause infections in open sores or wounds, and the heartworm larva is introduced into dogs by mosquitoes. Start by mixing 1 cup kerosene, 1 tablespoon castor oil, and 1 tablespoon mineral oil, then add 2 teaspoons eucalyptus oil and 1 cup trichloroethylene. Wipe on the animal's coat with a sponge, or, to use as a spray, mix with an equal amount of water and shake well each time you spray.

3.   Horse Hoof Grease

In the top of a double boiler heat 1 cup each of mineral oil, petrolatum, and paraffin wax just until the wax melts and the mixture can be stirred together. Cool until it starts to solidify and pour into cans. Apply with a fairly stiff brush.

4.   Salt Blocks

It is well known by now that any animal, including man, will seek out whatever is necessary to keep it going. Food and water are trivial examples. Children in slums have been found eating plaster off the walls because their diets were deficient in calcium. Those insane cravings that pregnant women sometimes get can usually be traced to some new mineral or vitamin that is being demanded by their bodies. Horses, cattle, and other animals will lick enough salt to satisfy their requirements. We can help them out by making it readily available, and salt blocks are quite easy to make. For a 40-pound block, use 20 pounds of ball clay and 20 pounds of coarse salt. Mix the clay with water until it is the consistency of putty and then mix in the salt, adding a little more water as you go to keep about the same consistency. Have a wooden box about one foot square handy to use as a mold, and allow the block to dry until it is hard.

$$H-\underset{\underset{H}{|}}{\overset{\overset{H}{|}}{C}}-\mathbf{5}-\underset{\underset{H}{|}}{\overset{\overset{H}{|}}{C}}-H$$

For Sports and Camping

If you have been to a park lately, almost any park, be it national, state, or city, you will have noticed that every year more and more Americans are taking to the great outdoors for any one or all of those physical and spiritual benefits to be found there. As this happens, more and more people are dismayed to find, miles from any habitation, tin cans, broken bottles, plastic cups, and other assorted garbage. The more people there are using an area, the more important it becomes to adhere to the new hiking and camping ethic. Don't trash up the landscape. If you've packed it in, pack it out. Take what you need with you, enjoy, and leave it in the condition you found it, if not better. With the new lightweight camp stoves there is no need even to gather wood for a fire, except in an emergency. For illumination, candles are still among the best things made, and beeswax, while more expensive, burns more slowly than paraffin wax and so is really more economical per hour of light. You can measure the rate of burning of a candle and if it burns 1/2 inch in an hour, say, you only need take a 1 1/2-inch stub for three hours of light and there is nothing left to pack out. There are many ways to economize in camping, as well as in other sports activities; here is a sampling.

1. *Insect Repellent*

At dusk, many insects appear that weren't there before. Most of these sleep during the daytime, and only become active at night. We tried to sleep on a beach that was beautiful in the daytime, but, without insect repellent, pure hell at night.

Into 1/2 cup denatured alcohol, mix 1 tablespoon each of camphor and calcium chloride, and stir until the camphor is dissolved. Take a small bottle of this with you to rub on exposed areas of skin.

2. *Easy Solid Fuel*

If you don't have a stove, these will do very nicely for out-of-door meals, and even if you do have a stove, it is always a good idea to have an emergency fuel supply on hand. These are lightweight and compact. Use light cardboard tubes such as those found inside rolls of toilet tissue, and cut them into 2-inch lengths. Close one end with a disc cut out of cardboard and held in place with a little tape. Now, depending on how many you want to make, melt a pound or more paraffin wax in the top of a double boiler and add fine sawdust, stirring it in well, until it is the consistency of very thick cream, or perhaps oatmeal is a better analogy. Let it cool until it just begins to solidify around the edges, give it a stir and fill the cardboard molds with it. When they are cool, melt a second batch of paraffin wax without sawdust this time, and dip the molds into this to coat the outsides. This way, the paper tube, when ignited, acts as a wick to start the inside burning.

3.   Ski Wax

Many jumpers and downhill racers have their own secret formulas for waxes to get the most speed under different snow conditions. Other people buy prepared wax, as fancy a brand as their pocketbooks will allow. You can save money and mystify your friends by using this good, all-purpose, homemade ski wax in a plain brown wrapper. Put 1 3/4 cups wood tar, 1/2 cup diglycol stearate and 1/4 cup carnauba wax in the top of a double boiler and heat until all is melted and you can stir it together. Allow it to cool off a little and pour it into molds. An excellent mold is a large size matchbox, the cardboard kind that kitchen matches come in.

4.   Gun Bluing

For the hunters and gun collectors among us, a gun that gets hard use may need to be reblued from time to time to replace that protective coating that prevents it from rusting. Into 1 1/2 cups water, mix 1/2 cup tannic acid, 1/2 cup antimony chloride and 3/4 cup ferric chloride. The part to be blued must be thoroughly clean and smooth. Apply with a fine brush, allow to dry, and apply a second coat. When that is dry, rub the metal with a cloth soaked in boiled linseed oil. (Caution: Antimony chloride is toxic.)

5.   Gun Cleaning Oil

Into 1 cup mineral oil, mix 1 tablespoon triethanolamine and 1 teaspoon denatured alcohol (any type). Use a few drops on the corner of a soft cloth.

104

6. Gun Lubricant

Many specialty stores, especially marine supply stores and gun shops, reflect that fact in their prices. For many items, merely being in a specialty store means that the price will be three times what it would if it were sold elsewhere. Specially made lubricants are no exception. Here is a perfectly good lubricant for the moving parts of your guns—or for any other fine mechanical equipment where high speeds and temperatures are not encountered in the moving parts, such as fishing equipment, camera equipment, tripods, and so on. It can be easily and inexpensively made by heating 3/4 cup petrolatum and 1/4 cup light machine oil in a double boiler until they can be mixed together. Let the mixture cool until it just starts to solidify and pour into containers.

7. Gun Barrel Cleaning Solvent

Of course guns are dangerous. No sane person would deny that. They can be mishandled and accidents do happen, often with tragic results. To minimize the possibility of such accidents observe the rules of etiquette for handling them, and keep them in as close to perfect working order as possible. Part of the routine for keeping them in good working order is to swab out the barrel after each use to keep it free of dirt and powder residue. What you want to use for that is a solution of 4 tablespoons motor oil (SAE 30), 2 tablespoons benzene, and 2 tablespoons amyl acetate. (Caution: Amyl acetate and benzene are flammable. Keep away from open flame. Avoid inhaling.)

8. Golf Ball Cleaner

Here is a simple and easy method for cleaning old golf balls. Soak them overnight in a solution of 1 cup water and 1/4 cup household ammonia. Rinse them off with clear water. Now you will be able to see them way off, two hundred yards or so down the fairway.

9. Golf Club Cleaner

To clean and polish heads and the metal shafts of your clubs, mix up 3/4 cup trisodium phosphate and 1/4 cup powdered alum. Dip a damp cloth or sponge in this powder, rub it on, rinse off with water, and dry.

10. Golf Club Grip Wax

Some people use a small cloth bag with powdered rosin in it to dust their hands when playing golf. This works well, but there is a tendency to use too much. Then it gums up, gets the grips dirty, and generally makes a mess. Just a little rosin dispersed in a hard wax is much more satisfactory, cleaner, and easier to use. Melt 4 tablespoons yellow beeswax in the top of a double boiler and add 1/2 teaspoon powdered rosin. Cool down slightly and pour into small molds which can be easily made from the cardboard tubes inside rolls of toilet tissue, or the small size cardboard matchboxes. As the wax is used the edge of the cardboard can be torn or cut away.

11. Making Your Own Golf Tees

This is so simple it's almost shameful, and why pay someone else to do something this easy? All you need is a polyethylene rod that is 3/16 inch in diameter. Cut it into 2-inch lengths and, holding one end gently with a pliers, suspend the other end in boiling water for a few seconds. When it is soft, press the end against a golf ball so that it expands slightly and takes the shape of the ball. Hold it in place for another few seconds until it cools. The other end can be sharpened with a pencil sharpener.

12. Net Preservative

You can give tennis and badminton nets protection against sun and damp, mildew and rot, by soaking them in a solution of 3 cups naphtha, 3/4 cup creosote, 1/4 cup fuel oil, and 5 ounces copper naphthenate. This is good both for untreated new nets and for prolonging the life of old ones. (Caution: All ingredient are toxic and flammable.)

$$H-\underset{\underset{H}{|}}{\overset{\overset{H}{|}}{C}}-6-\underset{\underset{H}{|}}{\overset{\overset{H}{|}}{C}}-H$$

Safety and First Aid

Nearly everyone follows basic safety rules every day, probably without even thinking about it. In the kitchen you exercise care when handling boiling liquids and hot things on the stove or in the oven. While driving a car you follow traffic regulations and rules of the road, which are all designed to keep traffic safe. And if you reflect for a moment, you know when it is that you have accidents. It's when you are in a hurry or distracted so that you fail to take the proper care in what you are doing or to notice the things that are going on around you. The times you grab a pot lid and burn your hand, or fail to check in the rear view mirror and back your car into a post, are times when you are trying to do too many things at once or when your mind is focused too intently on something other than what you are doing. This fact is the basis of all safety rules, wherever they occur, in kitchen, traffic, boating, swimming, in shop or garage or laboratory. The more potentially dangerous a situation is, the more elaborate the rules become. In the kitchen they are very general and rarely spelled out. In handling power tools they are more explicit. In handling weapons, safety rules are quite rigorous; and in handling atomic weapons they are explicit, precise, and absolutely inflexible.

These rules, of whatever degree, call our attention to the fact that in that situation we need to take care. If we store this general idea away in our heads, then, even in our more distracted moments, when we are in such a situation, a small signal will go off in our brain saying, "Now you are in a potentially dangerous situation, so to reduce the possibility of accident you had better pay attention."

Those are the general notions of safety. In addition, we would remind you of three specific safety instructions. First, read all labels carefully. Some are purely advertising, but some carry information required by law which is important for you to know and act upon. Second, to the best of your ability, keep dangerous materials out of the reach of children, and let them handle them only under close supervision. From our own experience we know, as we are sure you will too, that even teenagers can get flustered when doing something new for the first time; just recall your state of mind when you learned to drive an automobile. Third, be sure to have labels on all your preparations listing the ingredients, so if a small child or a pet does manage to get into something you will know what it contains.

With respect to first aid, we cannot urge too strongly that, if at all possible, you take the free courses offered by the National Red Cross. We all hope never to have an automobile accident, but we pay good money for insurance every year anyway. A Red Cross first-aid course is like free insurance. You hope never to use the knowledge, but if you do need it sometime, it is valuable. If it is impossible for you to take such a course, you can obtain a good first-aid handbook by writing to your local chapter of the Red Cross. They also offer a free Cardio-Pulmonary-Resuscitation course, or CPR course, which teaches the latest techniques of artificial respiration and closed-chest heart massage. Both of these are excellent, and, in our estimation, essential for everyone. The Red Cross also conducts free swimming classes in many areas of the country; that's another bit of free insurance you can give yourself, not to mention the gain in fun, health, and self-confidence that's in it. If you feel self-conscious about learning to swim at an advanced age, we have two words of advice for you. Overcome it. We have seen classes of youngsters two and three years old, classes of adults from forty to sixty or more years old as well as classes for those in between, and all have enjoyed and profited from the experience. No doubt most of them feel a little self-conscious at first, but when something is beneficial in so many ways, and could save your life, embarrassment should not stop you.

In virtually all major cities, and in thousands of not so major cities and towns, there are poison control centers that have telephones manned twenty-four hours a day. You should have that telephone number in a convenient and obvious place alongside those of the police, fire department, and doctor. They have files on the contents of all poisonous commercial products such as furniture polish, insecticides, and rat poisons, and can tell you the appropriate antidote to give immediately, and whether to induce vomiting or not.

Generally, vomiting should *not* be induced if the person has taken gasoline, kerosene, turpentine, strong acids or alkalis, or if he is unconscious. These substances cause more damage on the way up than they do in the stomach. If the victim can get down two large glasses of water or milk to help dilute the stuff, this will help. In most other cases, give the person two large glasses of water or milk and then induce vomiting. It is best to remove the poison in this way first, if you know what it is, and if the person is conscious. If he is not conscious he should be placed lying on his stomach with the head turned to one side. If he is conscious have him lie on his back, keep him warm, and then call your doctor or the poison control center. Do not leave the person alone, and be prepared to start mouth-to-mouth resuscitation at the first sign of difficulty in breathing. Recovery can come after hours of artificial respiration, so do not give up. If you are alone and need to call for help, you can stop just long enough to dial the phone. It may be a little tricky holding the phone and giving mouth-to-mouth resuscitation at the same time, but it can be done.

A handy substance to have around the house, and that you can make rather easily, is a universal antidote powder. It consists of 2 parts activated charcoal, 1 part magnesium oxide, and 1 part tannic acid. You can make it in an emergency using burnt toast for the charcoal, milk of magnesia, and instant tea powder for the magnesium and the tannic acid. Give two tablespoons of this in half a glass of warm water. Much of the above information was obtained from *The Merck Manual of Diagnosis and Therapy* and used here with their kind permission.

We would like to repeat, if you are interested in safety and first aid, by far the best thing to do is to take the free Red Cross courses given in most cities and towns. They are usually offered at convenient times in the evening, they are interesting, and they have enabled many people to save lives.

One final and important reminder on safety. When you make a chemical product, *always* label the container, not only as to what the product is, but also the ingredients. In this way, should a child inadvertently consume some of it, your doctor will know what to prescribe as an antidote.

APPENDIX A

Formula Ingredients and Their Metric Equivalents

The metric equivalents and specific gravity of the ingredients have been rounded off for simplified home use. For laboratory and other work requiring precise measurements, recalculations should be made to insure exactitude.

ACNE LOTION

Isopropyl alcohol	4 tablespoons	60.0 ml
Distilled water	1/2 cup	118.0 ml
Glycerin	1 1/2 teaspoons	7.0 ml
Triethanolamine	1/8 teaspoon	0.8 ml
Perfume	to suit	

ADDITIVE FOR HEAVILY SOILED LAUNDRY

Mason sand	5 cups	1.2 kg
Soda ash	3 cups	720.0 grams

AFTER-SHAVE LOTION

Witch hazel	1/4 cup	60.0 ml
Boric acid	1/4 teaspoon	1.0 grams
Glycerin	5 tablespoons	75.0 ml
Denatured alcohol	1/4 cup	60.0 ml
Water	1 cup	240.0 ml
Perfume	to suit	
Powdered alum	1/2 teaspoon	2.4 grams

Formula Ingredients and Their Metric Equivalents

ALCOHOL RESISTANT FINISH FOR WOOD

Paraffin oil	3 cups	720.0 ml
Vinegar	1 tablespoon	15.0 ml

ALCOHOL SOLID FUEL

Denatured alcohol	2 cups	480.0 ml
Caustic soda	1 1/2 teaspoons	7.5 grams
Stearic acid	1/8 cup	30.0 ml

ALGAE SPRAY FOR PONDS

Sodium penta-chlorophenate	1 gallon	4.0 liters
Water	5 gallons	20.0 liters

ALLOVER SKIN CREAM

Anhydrous lanolin	3/4 tablespoon	11.0 grams
White petrolatum	1 cup	240.0 grams
Water	2 cups	480.0 ml
Glycerin	1 teaspoon	5.0 ml
Perfume	to suit	

ALL-PURPOSE GERMICIDAL CREAM

White petrolatum	1/2 cup	120.0 grams
Mineral oil	3/8 cup	90.0 ml
Beeswax	1/8 cup	30.0 ml
Water	1/4 cup	60.0 ml
Borax	1 tablespoon	15.0 grams
Parachloro-metacresol	1 tablespoon	15.0 grams

ALMONDS, LEMONS, AND LIMES CREAM

Almond oil	1/8 teaspoon	0.5 ml
Glycerin	1/8 teaspoon	0.5 ml
Lemon oil	1/8 teaspoon	0.5 ml
Lime water	1 cup	240.0 ml

ALUMINUM CLEANER

Powdered alum	2 tablespoons	30.0 grams
Trisodium phosphate	1 cup	230.0 grams

ALUMINUM POLISH

Powdered alum	1/2 cup	120.0 grams
Whiting	3/4 cup	180.0 grams
Talc	1/2 cup	120.0 grams

AMERICAN MOUTHWASH

Sodium bicarbonate	2 tablespoons	30.0 grams
Borax	1 tablespoon	15.0 grams
Zinc chloride	1/8 teaspoon	0.6 grams
Menthol crystals	1 speck	
Denatured alcohol (type 37)	1/2 cup	120.0 ml
Glycerin	1 cup	240.0 ml
Cinnamon oil	to suit	
Water	4 cups	960.0 ml
Red food coloring	to suit	

Formula Ingredients and Their Metric Equivalents

AMMONIA CLEANING POWDER

Powdered hard soap	2 cups	450.0 grams
Ammonium carbonate	2 cups	450.0 grams

ANTACID LIQUID

Sodium bicarbonate	1 tablespoon	15.0 grams
Sugar	1 teaspoon	5.0 grams
Peppermint Oil	5 drops	1.5 ml
Water	1 cup	240.0 ml

ANT EXTERMINATOR

Molasses syrup	1/2 cup	120.0 ml
Sugar	1/4 cup	60.0 grams
Dry yeast	1/4 cup	60.0 grams

ANTIFOG PREPARATION

Silicone liquid emulsion	1 tablespoon	15.0 ml
Water	3 cups	700.0 ml

ANTIPERSPIRANT LIQUID

Powdered alum	1 tablespoon	15.0 grams
Zinc oxide (powdered)	1 tablespoon	15.0 grams
Denatured alcohol	1/2 cup	120.0 ml
Water	2 1/2 cups	600.0 ml

Appendix A

ANTIRUST TOOL COATING

| Lanolin | 1 cup | 250.0 grams |
| Petrolatum | 1 cup | 250.0 grams |

ANT MOUND ERADICATOR

Pyrethrin	1 teaspoon	5.0 ml
Liquid soap	1/4 cup	60.0 ml
Water	2 gallons	8.0 liters

ASTRINGENT LOTION

Water	3 cups	700.0 ml
Glycerin	1 tablespoon	15.0 ml
Alum	2 tablespoons	30.0 grams

ATHLETE'S FOOT POWDER

Sodium thio-sulfate (powdered)	1/3 cup	80.0 grams
Boric acid (powdered)	1 cup	240.0 grams
Talc	2/3 cup	160.0 grams

BABY OIL

| White mineral oil (U.S.P. grade) | 1 pint | 480.0 ml |
| Perfume | as desired | |

Formula Ingredients and Their Metric Equivalents

BASIC SOAP

Lye flakes (caustic soda)	13 ounces	390.0 grams
Tallow	6 pounds	2.7 kg
Cold water	5 cups	1.2 liters
Perfume	to suit	

BATTERY TERMINAL PROTECTIVE COATING

Sodium silicate	1 cup	240.0 grams
Water	1 cup	240.0 ml

BEAUTY MASK

Clay	4 cups	1.0 kg
Talc	1 cup	240.0 grams
Titanium dioxide	1/8 cup	30.0 grams

BED BUG EXTERMINATOR

Powdered alum	3/4 cup	180.0 grams
Boric acid (powdered)	2 tablespoons	30.0 grams
Salicylic acid	2 tablespoons	30.0 grams

BLOND HAIR RINSE

Tincture of rhubarb	2 1/2 tablespoons	37.5 ml
Isopropyl alcohol	1/3 cup	80.0 ml
Propylene glycol	2 teaspoons	10.0 ml
Water	3 3/4 cups	900.0 ml
Perfume	to suit	

BODY AND FACE POWDER

Talc	2 cups	480.0 grams
Boric acid	2 tablespoons	30.0 grams
Cornstarch	1/2 cup	120.0 grams
Dye	to suit	
Perfume	to suit	

BOOK COVER COATING

White shellac	1 pint	500.0 ml
Denatured alcohol	1 pint	500.0 ml

BOTTLE AND JAR CLEANER

Caustic soda	5 tablespoons	70.0 grams
Sodium aluminate	1 teaspoon	5.0 grams
Water	1 gallon	4.0 liters

BRASS POLISH

Stearic acid or powdered paraffin	3/4 tablespoon	12.0 grams
Petroleum distillate	1/4 cup	50.0 grams
Caustic soda	1/2 tablespoon	8.0 grams
Denatured alcohol	1 tablespoon	15.0 ml
Clay or talc to make paste		

BUBBLE BATH

Sodium lauryl sulfate	1 3/4 cups	400.0 grams

Formula Ingredients and Their Metric Equivalents

Sodium sesquicarbonate	3 cups	680.0 grams
Sodium alginate	1 teaspoon	5.0 grams
Perfume (type 2)	to suit	

CANDLES

Paraffin wax	2 cups	480.0 grams
Stearic acid	1 cup	240.0 grams
Cotton wicking		
Molds		

CAR LIQUID WAX

Yellow beeswax (powdered)	2 tablespoons	30.0 grams
Ceresin wax (powdered)	1/2 cup	120.0 grams
Turpentine	2 cups	480.0 ml
Pine oil	1 tablespoon	15.0 ml

CAR PASTE WAX

Yellow beeswax (powdered)	2 tablespoons	30.0 grams
Ceresin wax (powdered)	5 tablespoons	75.0 grams
Carnauba wax (powdered)	9 tablespoons	130.0 grams
Montan wax (powdered)	3 tablespoons	42.0 grams
Mineral oil	2 cups	480.0 ml
Turpentine	4 tablespoons	60.0 ml
Pine oil	1 tablespoon	15.0 ml

Appendix A

CAR SOAP

Corn oil	2 cups	480.0 ml
Caustic potash (flaked)	3 tablespoons	45.0 grams
Water	1 cup	240.0 ml

CARPENTER ANT EXTERMINATOR

Paradichloro-benzene (moth crystals)	2 cups	460.0 grams
Kerosene	2 quarts	2.0 liters

CARPET CLEANER

Whole-wheat flour	3 cups	1.4 kg
Mineral oil	1 1/2 cups	360.0 ml
Aluminum stearate	1 tablespoon	15.0 grams
Salicylic acid	1 tablespoon	15.0 grams
Water	1 1/4 cups	300.0 ml

CHARCOAL LIGHTER

Mineral oil	2 3/4 cups	650.0 ml
Kerosene	1/4 cup	60.0 ml

CHIMNEY SOOT REMOVER

Salt	1 cup	240.0 grams
Zinc oxide powder	1 cup	240.0 grams

Formula Ingredients and Their Metric Equivalents

COCKROACH EXTERMINATER

Borax	4 tablespoons	60.0 grams
Flour	2 tablespoons	30.0 grams
Cocoa powder	1 tablespoon	15.0 grams

COLD CREAM

Mineral oil	2 cups	480.0 ml
White beeswax	1/2 cup	120.0 grams
Borax (powdered)	1 1/2 tablespoons	22.0 grams
Water	1 cup	240.0 ml

COLOGNE

Ethyl alcohol (vodka)	1 cup	240.0 ml
Lemon oil	17 drops	5.0 ml
Bergamot oil	7 drops	2.0 ml
Neroli oil	40 drops	12.0 ml
Rosemary oil	7 drops	2.0 ml

COMB AND HAIRBRUSH CLEANER

Household ammonia	1 tablespoon	15.0 ml
Water	2 cups	480.0 ml

CONCRETE CLEANER

Sodium metasilicate	3 1/4 cups	740.0 grams
Trisodium phosphate	3/4 cup	180.0 grams
Soda ash	1/2 cup	120.0 grams

Appendix A

CONCRETE DUSTPROOFER

Sodium silicate	1 quart	1.0 liters
Water	4 quarts	4.0 liters

CONTACT LENS FLUID

Sodium bicarbonate	1/8 teaspoon	0.8 gram
Salt	1/8 teaspoon	0.8 gram
Water (distilled)	1/2 cup	120.0 ml

COOLING HAND LOTION

Menthol crystals	1/8 teaspoon	0.6 gram
Glycerin	1/4 cup	60.0 ml
Denatured alcohol	1 1/2 cups	360.0 ml
Water	3/4 cup	180.0 ml
Perfume	to suit	

COSMETIC REMOVER

Yellow beeswax	1/2 cup	120.0 grams
Paraffin wax	1/3 cup	80.0 grams
Mineral oil	1 cup	240.0 ml

CREAM FOR CHAPPED LIPS

Beeswax	1/4 cup	60.0 grams
Castor oil	1/4 cup	60.0 ml
Sesame oil	3 tablespoons	40.0 ml
Anhydrous lanolin	2 tablespoons	30.0 ml

122

Formula Ingredients and Their Metric Equivalents

CUCUMBER SKIN LOTION

Cucumber juice	4 cups	960.0 ml
Glycerin	1 cup	240.0 ml
Isopropyl alcohol	1/4 cup	60.0 ml
Benzoic acid	1 speck	
Rose oil	to suit	

DANDELION PLANT KILLER

Kerosene	1 gallon	4.0 liters
Denatured alcohol	1 pint	500.0 ml
Furfuraldehyde	1 pound	450.0 grams

DANDELION ROOT KILLER

Kerosene	1 gallon	4.0 liters
Paraffin oil	1 cup	250.0 ml

DENTURE ADHESIVE

Boric acid	1 1/2 teaspoons	7.5 grams
Tragacanth (powdered)	1/2 cup	120.0 grams
Acacia (powdered)	2 tablespoons	30.0 grams

DEODORANT CREAM

Stearic acid (powdered)	1/4 cup	60.0 grams
Water	3 1/2 cups	800.0 ml
Triethanolamine	2 tablespoons	30.0 ml
Powdered alum	2 tablespoons	30.0 grams

Appendix A

DEODORANT POWDER

Alum	1 tablespoon	15.0 grams
Boric acid	1/4 cup	60.0 grams
Talc	1/3 cup	80.0 grams
Perfume	to suit	

DISHWASHER DETERGENT

Soda ash	1 cup	240.0 grams
Sodium metasilicate	2 cups	480.0 grams
Trisodium phosphate	1 cup	240.0 grams

DISINFECTANT

Cresylic acid	1 1/4 cups	300.0 ml
Sulfonated castor oil	2/3 cup	160.0 ml
Oleic acid	3 tablespoons	45.0 ml
Caustic soda	1 teaspoon	5.0 grams
Water	1/2 cup	120.0 ml

DRAIN CLEANER

Baking soda	1 cup	240.0 grams
Salt	1 cup	240.0 grams
Cream of tartar	1/4 cup	60.0 grams

DRAIN OPENER

Caustic soda	3/4 cup	180.0 grams
Calcium carbonate	1 cup	240.0 grams
Caustic potash	3 cups	720.0 grams

Formula Ingredients and Their Metric Equivalents

ELECTRIC AFTER-SHAVE LOTION

Witch hazel	1/4 cup	60.0 ml
Denatured alcohol	1/4 cup	60.0 ml
Powdered alum	1/2 teaspoon	2.0 grams
Boric acid	1/4 teaspoon	1.0 gram
Glycerin	5 tablespoons	75.0 ml
Water	1 cup	240.0 ml
Perfume	to suit	

ELECTRIC PRE-SHAVE LOTION

Denatured alcohol	1 cup	240.0 ml
Glycerin	2 tablespoons	30.0 ml
Water	3/4 cup	180.0 ml
Perfume	to suit	

ENGINE AND PARTS DEGREASING COMPOUND

Trisodium phosphate	3 1/2 cups	800.0 grams
Sodium bicarbonate	1 cup	240.0 grams
Sodium metasilicate	1/2 cup	120.0 grams

EXTRACTS OF SPECIAL FLAVORS

Almond or other oil	15 drops	5.0 ml
Ethyl alcohol (vodka)	1/4 cup	60.0 ml
Water	1/4 cup	60.0 ml

Appendix A

FABRIC SOFTENER

Lauryl pyridin-ium chloride	4 cups	960.0 grams
Denatured alcohol	1 cup	240.0 ml
Water	1/3 cup	80.0 ml

FENCE POST PRESERVATIVE

Water	1 gallon	4.0 liters
Zinc chloride	1 3/4 pounds	800.0 grams

FERTILIZER FOR AZALEAS

Ammonium sulfate	1 1/3 cups	300.0 grams
Superphosphate	1 1/2 cups	340.0 grams
Potash	9 cups	2.0 kg
Sawdust	1 bushel	8.0 kg

FERTILIZER FOR HOUSE PLANTS

Sodium phos-phate (tribasic)	3 ounces	90.0 grams
Potassium nitrate	4 ounces	120.0 grams

FINGERNAIL HARDENER

Powdered alum	1 teaspoon	5.0 grams
Glycerin	1 tablespoon	15.0 ml
Water	3 tablespoons	45.0 ml

Formula Ingredients and Their Metric Equivalents

FINGERNAIL SOFTENER

Triethanolamine	3 tablespoons	45.0 ml
Castor oil or olive oil	2 tablespoons	30.0 ml
Water	1/2 cup	120.0 ml

FIRE EXTINGUISHER

Soda ash	2 cups	480.0 grams
Alum	1 cup	240.0 grams
Borax	3/4 cup	180.0 grams
Potash	1/4 cup	60.0 grams
Sodium silicate	3 pints	1.4 liters

FIREPLACE STARTER

Sawdust	5 pounds	2.5 kg
Fuel or auto drain oil	1 quart	1.0 liter

FIREPROOFING CHRISTMAS TREES

Ammonium sulfate	1 cup	240.0 grams
Boric acid	1/2 cup	120.0 grams
Borax	2 tablespoons	30.0 grams
Water	1 gallon	4.0 liters

FIREPROOFING CLOTH

Ammonium phosphate	1/2 cup	120.0 grams
Ammonium chloride	1 cup	240.0 grams
Water	3 pints	1.4 liters

Appendix A

FIREPROOFING WOOD

Zinc chloride	1/2 cup	120.0 grams
Ferric chloride	1/4 cup	60.0 grams
Boric acid	3 tablespoons	45.0 grams
Ammonium phosphate	3 tablespoons	45.0 grams
Water	2 quarts	2.0 liters

FLEA SOAP

Kerosene	5 cups	1.2 liters
Oleic acid	1/2 cup	120.0 ml
Triethanolamine	1/4 cup	60.0 ml

FLOOR MOP OIL

Mineral oil	2 cups	480.0 ml
Turpentine	1 cup	240.0 ml

FLOOR POLISH (LIQUID)

Paraffin	1/4 cup	60.0 grams
Mineral oil	2 quarts	2.0 liters

FLOOR SWEEPING COMPOUND

Sawdust (sifted)	12 cups	3.0 kg
Rock salt	4 cups	1.0 kg
Mineral oil	3 cups	720.0 ml

Formula Ingredients and Their Metric Equivalents

FLY SPRAY

Deodorized		
kerosene	7 cups	1.7 liters
Pyrethrin	3/4 cup	180.0 ml
Methyl salicylate	1 tablespoon	15.0 ml

FOAMING DENTURE CLEANER

Sodium perborate	1 tablespoon	15.0 grams
Water (hot)	1 cup	240.0 ml

FUEL IMPROVER FOR OIL FURNACES

Naphthalene	90 ounces	2.7 liters
Anthracene	10 ounces	300.0 ml

FURNITURE FINISHING POLISH

Turpentine	1 cup	240.0 ml
Mineral oil	1 cup	240.0 ml
Rottenstone powder (fine)	1 tablespoon	15.0 grams

FURNITURE LEMON OIL POLISH

Mineral oil	1 quart	1.0 liters
Lemon oil	1 tablespoon	15.0 ml

FURNITURE SILICONE POLISH

Silicone oil	1 tablespoon	15.0 ml
Mineral oil	2 cups	480.0 ml

Appendix A

FURNITURE THIN FILM POLISH

Mineral oil	1 1/2 cups	360.0 ml
Benzene	1 cup	240.0 ml

FURNITURE WATER EMULSION POLISH

Mineral oil	1 1/4 cups	300.0 ml
Steam distilled pine oil	1 tablespoon	15.0 ml
Liquid detergent	4 tablespoons	60.0 ml
Water	1 1/2 cups	360.0 ml

FURNITURE WAX POLISH

Mineral oil	2 cups	480.0 ml
Carnauba wax	1 tablespoon	15.0 grams

GALVANIZED COATING REPAIR

Powdered zinc	1/2 tablespoon	8.0 grams
Powdered lead	1/4 tablespoon	4.0 grams
Powdered tin	6 tablespoons	90.0 grams

GARAGE FLOOR CLEANER

Powdered soap	3 cups	700.0 grams
Sodium metasilicate	6 tablespoons	90.0 grams

GARDEN INSECTICIDE

Pyrethrin	1 cup	240.0 ml
Kerosene or fuel oil	2 quarts	2.0 liters
Water	2 quarts	2.0 liters
Liquid detergent	1/4 cup	60.0 ml

Formula Ingredients and Their Metric Equivalents

GASOLINE ANTI-KNOCK ADDITIVE

Benzene	1/2 cup	120.0 ml
Denatured alcohol	1 cup	240.0 ml
Hydrogen peroxide	1 tablespoon	15.0 ml

GASOLINE ENGINE CLEANING ADDITIVES

Motor oil (SAE 30)	1 cup	240.0 ml
Paraffin	1 cup	240.0 grams

GLASS SCRATCH REMOVER

Iron oxide (jeweler's rouge)	1 ounce	30.0 grams
Glycerin	1 ounce	30.0 ml
Water	1 ounce	30.0 ml

GLASS SPRAY CLEANER

Denatured alcohol	1 cup	240.0 ml
Lactic acid	5 drops	1.5 ml
Water	2 cups	480.0 ml

GLYCERIN SKIN GEL

Gelatin	5 teaspoons	20.0 grams
Glycerin	3 tablespoons	45.0 ml
Water	2 1/4 cups	540.0 ml
Perfume	to suit	

GOLD POLISH

Fuller's earth	1/2 cup	120.0 grams
Calcium carbonate	1/2 cup	120.0 grams
Ammonium sulfate	1 tablespoon	15.0 grams
Aluminum powder	1 teaspoon	5.0 grams

Appendix A

GOLF BALL CLEANER

Household ammonia	1/4 cup	60.0 ml
Water	1 cup	240.0 ml

GOLF CLUB CLEANER

Powdered alum	1/4 cup	60.0 grams
Trisodium phosphate	3/4 cup	180.0 grams

GOLF CLUB GRIP WAX

Yellow beeswax	4 tablespoons	60.0 grams
Rosin	1/2 teaspoon	2.5 grams

GRASS KILLER

Calcium chloride	1 pound	460.0 grams
Water	1 gallon	4.0 liters

GUN BARREL CLEANING SOLVENT

Amyl acetate	2 tablespoons	30.0 ml
Benzene	2 tablespoons	30.0 ml
Motor oil (SAE 30)	4 tablespoons	60.0 ml

GUN BLUING

Ferric chloride	3/4 cup	180.0 grams
Antimony chloride	1/2 cup	120.0 grams
Tannic acid	1/2 cup	120.0 grams
Water	1 1/2 cups	360.0 ml
Boiled linseed oil		

132

Formula Ingredients and Their Metric Equivalents

GUN CLEANING OIL

Mineral oil	1 cup	240.0 ml
Triethanolamine	1 tablespoon	15.0 ml
Denatured alcohol	1 teaspoon	5.0 ml

GUN LUBRICANT

Petrolatum	3/4 cup	180.0 grams
Light machine oil	1/4 cup	60.0 ml

HAIR CONDITIONING CREAM

Stearic acid	3/4 tablespoon	12.0 grams
Petrolatum	1/4 cup	60.0 grams
Lanolin	1 teaspoon	5.0 grams
Triethanolamine	1 teaspoon	5.0 ml
Water	1/2 cup	120.0 ml
Perfume	to suit	

HAIR SET SPRAY

Acacia	1/2 teaspoon	2.5 grams
Borax	1 teaspoon	5.0 grams
Denatured alcohol	6 tablespoons	90.0 ml
Warm water	2 cups	480.0 ml
Perfume	to suit	

HAIR TONIC

Oxyquinoline sulfate	1 teaspoon	5.0 grams
Isopropyl alcohol	4 tablespoons	60.0 ml
Distilled water	3 cups	720.0 ml
Perfume	to suit	

Appendix A

HAIR WAVE LOTION

Tragacanth gum	1/2 teaspoon	2.21 grams
Isopropyl alcohol	1/2 cup	120.0 ml
Water	1 1/2 cups	360.0 ml
Potassium carbonate	2 teaspoons	10.0 grams
Borax	1/2 teaspoon	2.5 grams
Perfume	to suit	

HAND CLEANER FOR GREASE AND GRIME

Diglycol laurate	1/4 cup	60.0 ml
Mineral oil	1 cup	240.0 ml

HEAVY-DUTY HAND SOAP

Water	1 cup	240.0 ml
Kerosene	1 cup	240.0 ml
Oleic acid	5 teaspoons	25.0 ml
Triethanolamine	2 1/2 teaspoons	12.5 ml

HONEY AND ALMOND LOTION

Stearic acid	1 1/2 tablespoons	22.5 grams
Ethylene glycol	2 tablespoons	30.0 ml
Glycerin	6 tablespoons	90.0 ml
Honey	2 teaspoons	10.0 ml
Water	2 cups	480.0 ml
Almond oil	to suit	

HORSE HOOF GREASE

Mineral oil	1 cup	240.0 ml
Petrolatum	1 cup	240.0 grams
Paraffin wax	1 cup	240.0 grams

Formula Ingredients and Their Metric Equivalents

HOUSEHOLD AMMONIA

Ammonium hydroxide	3/4 cup	180.0 ml
Water	1 gallon	4.0 liters

HOUSEHOLD AMMONIA SUBSTITUTE

Trisodium phosphate	6 tablespoons	90.0 grams
Lauryl pyridinium chloride	1/2 tablespoon	7.5 grams
Water	1 gallon	4.0 liters

INSECT REPELLENT

Camphor	1 tablespoon	15.0 grams
Calcium chloride	1 tablespoon	15.0 grams
Denatured alcohol	1/2 cup	120.0 ml

INSECT REPELLENT FOR ANIMALS

Trichloroethylene	1 cup	240.0 ml
Kerosene	1 cup	240.0 ml
Castor oil	1 tablespoon	15.0 ml
Mineral oil	1 tablespoon	15.0 ml
Eucalyptus oil	2 teaspoons	10.0 ml

INK SPOT REMOVER

Sodium perborate	1/2 teaspoon	2.5 grams
Water	1/2 cup	120.0 ml

Appendix A

JAPANESE BEETLE SPRAY FOR TREES AND BUSHES

Alum	5 ounces	150.0 grams
Hydrated lime	2 pounds	900.0 grams
Water	10 gallons	40.0 liters

JAR AND BOTTLE SEALER

Gelatin	1 teaspoon	5.0 grams
Water	1 cup	240.0 ml
Glycerin	3 tablespoons	45.0 ml

LAUNDRY BLEACH

Chlorinated lime	2 cups	480.0 grams
Sodium carbonate	3 cups	720.0 grams
Water	1 gallon	4.0 liters

LAUNDRY BLUING

Ultramarine blue	1/4 teaspoon	1.0 grams
Sodium bicarbonate	1 3/4 cups	400.0 grams
Corn syrup	1/2 cup	120.0 ml

LAUNDRY DETERGENT

Lauryl pyridinium chloride	3 3/4 cups	900.0 grams
Sodium dodecyl benzene sulfate	2 1/2 cups	600.0 grams
Sodium tripolyphosphate	10 1/2 cups	2.5 kg
Sodium bicarbonate	8 cups	1.9 kg

136

Formula Ingredients and Their Metric Equivalents

LAUNDRY STARCH

Cornstarch	1 cup	240.0 grams
Wheat starch	1/2 cup	120.0 grams

LEAK SEAL FOR TIRES

Liquid latex emulsion	1 cup	240.0 ml
Sodium silicate	1/2 cup	120.0 ml

LEATHER PRESERVATIVE

Neat's-foot oil	1/2 cup	120.0 ml
Castor oil	1/2 cup	120.0 ml

LEMON HAIR RINSE

Lemon oil	10 drops	3.0 ml
Isopropyl alcohol	1 cup	240.0 ml
Citric acid	2 tablespoons	30.0 grams
Tartaric acid	4 tablespoons	60.0 grams
Water	1 1/2 cups	360.0 ml

LENS CLEANER

Potassium oleate	2 tablespoons	30.0 grams
Glycerin	1 tablespoon	15.0 ml
Turpentine	1/4 teaspoon	2.0 ml

LIBRARY GLUE

Yellow dextrin	4 tablespoons	60.0 grams
Calcium chloride	2 tablespoons	30.0 grams
Water	2 cups	480.0 ml

Appendix A

LIGHTER FLUID

Deodorized naphtha	2 cups	480.0 ml
Citronella oil	1/8 teaspoon	0.5 ml

LINOLEUM POLISH

Carnauba wax	1/2 cup	120.0 grams
Paraffin wax	2 tablespoons	30.0 grams
Yellow beeswax	4 tablespoons	60.0 grams
Turpentine	4 cups	960.0 ml

LIQUID DETERGENT FOR DISHWASHING

Sodium metaphosphate	1 cup	240.0 grams
Trisodium phosphate	3 cups	720.0 grams

LIQUID MASCARA

Tincture of benzoin (25%)	4 tablespoons	60.0 ml
Black dye	to suit	

LUBRICATING OIL

Paraffin oil	1 quart	1.0 liter
Rape seed oil	3 ounces	90.0 ml

MARBLE CLEANING POWDER

Sodium sulfate	3/4 cup	180.0 grams
Sodium sulfite	1/4 cup	60.0 grams

138

Formula Ingredients and Their Metric Equivalents

METAL CLEANER

Trisodium phosphate	3/4 cup	180.0 grams
Soda ash	3 cups	720.0 grams
Baking soda	1 1/4 cups	300.0 grams

METAL POLISH

Diatomaceous earth	1 cup	240.0 grams
Household ammonia	1/2 cup	120.0 ml
Denatured alcohol	1/2 cup	120.0 ml
Water		

MILDEWPROOFING

Copper naphthenate	2 cups	480.0 grams
Amyl acetate	1/4 cup	60.0 ml
Zinc bromide	3/4 cup	180.0 grams

MILDEWPROOFING PAINT

Zinc oxide	19 ounces	570.0 grams
Mercuric chloride	1/2 ounce	15.0 grams
Linseed oil	7 1/2 ounces	225.0 ml

MINERAL OIL EMULSION FOR TILE FLOORS

Mineral oil	4 cups	960.0 ml
Ammonium oleate	6 tablespoons	90.0 grams
Water	3 cups	720.0 ml

Appendix A

MODELING CLAY

Cornstarch	1 cup	240.0 grams
Bicarbonate of soda	2 cups	480.0 grams
Cold water	1 1/2 cups	360.0 ml
Food coloring	if desired	

MOISTURE PROTECTION

Silica gel	1/2 cup	120.0 grams

MOLD STAIN REMOVER

Distilled water	3/4 cup	180.0 ml
Household ammonia	1 teaspoon	5.0 ml
Hydrogen peroxide	4 tablespoons	60.0 ml

MOTHPROOFING

Ammonium selenate	1 teaspoon	5.0 grams
Water	1 gallon	4.0 liters

MOUSE AND RAT HOLE SEALER

Asphalt	1 1/2 cups	360.0 grams
Kerosene	1 1/4 cups	300.0 ml
Powdered asbestos	2 cups	480.0 grams

NET PRESERVATIVE

Copper naphthenate	5 ounces	150.0 grams

140

Formula Ingredients and Their Metric Equivalents

Fuel oil	1/4 cup	60.0 ml
Creosote	3/4 cup	180.0 ml
Naphtha	3 cups	720.0 ml

NONFOAMING DENTURE CLEANER

Citric acid	1 teaspoon	5.0 grams
Isopropyl alcohol	1 cup	240.0 ml
Peppermint oil	10 drops	3.0 ml

OIL FOR LAMPS AND TORCHES

Kerosene	1 gallon	4.0 liters
Mineral lime	3 ounces	90.0 grams
Dye	to suit	

OVEN CLEANER

Trisodium phosphate	1/2 cup	120.0 grams
Soda ash	1/2 cup	120.0 grams
Sodium perborate	1 cup	240.0 grams
Powdered soap	2 tablespoons	30.0 grams

PAINT AND VARNISH REMOVER

Caustic soda	1 cup	240.0 grams
Caustic potash	3/4 cup	180.0 grams
Calcium carbonate	2 cups	480.0 grams
Pumice powder	1 1/2 cups	360.0 grams

PAINT BRUSH CLEANER

Household ammonia	1/4 cup	60.0 ml

Denatured alcohol	1/4 cup	60.0 ml
Kerosene	4 cups	960.0 ml
Oleic acid	2 cups	480.0 ml

PAINT SPOT REMOVER

| Turpentine | 1 cup | 240.0 ml |
| Household ammonia | 1 cup | 240.0 ml |

PERSPIRATION STAIN REMOVER

| Sodium perborate | 3 tablespoons | 45.0 grams |
| Water | 2 cups | 480.0 ml |

PETROLEUM JELLY

White petrolatum	1/2 cup	120.0 grams
Paraffin wax	3 tablespoons	45.0 grams
Mineral oil	2 cups	480.0 ml

POLISHING CLOTH

Silicone water emulsion	1 tablespoon	15.0 ml
Water	1 cup	240.0 ml
12"×12" flannel cloth		

PORCELAIN CLEANER

| Sodium sulfite | 1/4 cup | 60.0 grams |
| Sodium sulfate | 3/4 cup | 180.0 grams |

Formula Ingredients and Their Metric Equivalents

PRESERVING CUT FLOWERS

Granulated sugar	1 cup	240.0 grams
Silver nitrate	20 drops	6.0 ml

RABBIT REPELLENT

Denatured alcohol	1 quart	1.0 liters
Gum rosin	1 cup	240.0 grams

RADIATOR CLEANER

Washing soda	2 1/2 cups	600.0 grams
Warm water	3 quarts	3.0 liters

RADIATOR LEAK SEALER

Sulfite liquor	1 cup	240.0 ml
Asbestos powder	1/8 cup	25.0 grams
Water	7/8 cup	200.0 ml

RADIATOR RUST REMOVER

Sodium bisulfite	4 ounces	120.0 grams
Oxalic acid	4 ounces	120.0 grams
Water	2 gallons	8.0 liters

RADIATOR SCALE PREVENTER

Sodium silicate	3 ounces	90.0 ml
Trisodium phosphate	1 ounce	30.0 grams
Water	1 gallon	4.0 liters

RADIATOR SCALE REMOVER

Trisodium phosphate	6 ounces	180.0 grams
Water	4 gallons	16.0 liters

REFRESHING FACE WASH

Denatured alcohol	3/4 cup	180.0 ml
Witch hazel	6 tablespoons	90.0 ml
Glycerin	4 tablespoons	60.0 ml
Perfume	to suit	

REFRIGERATOR DEODORIZER

Activated charcoal	1/4 cup	60.0 grams
Calcium carbonate	1/4 cup	60.0 grams
Portland cement	1 cup	240.0 grams
Vermiculite	1/2 cup	120.0 grams
Powdered aluminum	2 teaspoons	10.0 grams

REMOVING WATER SPOTS FROM FURNITURE

Lemon oil	10 drops	3.0 ml
Denatured alcohol	1 pint	500.0 ml

ROOT DESTROYER FOR DRAINS

Caustic soda	3 cups	720.0 grams
Copper sulfate	1/4 cup	60.0 grams
Ammonium sulfate	1 teaspoon	5.0 grams

Formula Ingredients and Their Metric Equivalents

RUBBING ALCOHOL

Denatured alcohol	2 cups	480.0 ml
Glycerin	1/2 teaspoon	3.0 ml
Castor oil	1/2 teaspoon	3.0 ml

RUST STAIN REMOVER

Potassium persulfate	3/4 ounce	23.0 grams
Water	1 pint	500.0 ml

SADDLE SOAP

Soap powder	3/4 cup	180.0 grams
Water	3 1/2 cups	840.0 ml
Neat's-foot oil	1/4 cup	60.0 ml
Beeswax	1/2 cup	120.0 grams

SALT BLOCKS

Coarse salt	20 pounds	9.6 kg
Ball clay	20 pounds	9.6 kg
Water	as needed	

SEPTIC TANK REACTIVATOR

Brown sugar	1 pound	450.0 grams
Dried yeast	1 envelope	
Water	1 quart	1.0 liter

Appendix A

SHAMPOO

Oleic acid	1 1/4 cups	300.0 ml
Coconut oil	1 cup	240.0 ml
Triethanolamine	1 1/4 cups	300.0 ml
Perfume	to suit	

SILVER POLISH

Water	1 1/2 cups	360.0 ml
Stearic acid	2 tablespoons	30.0 grams
Soda ash	1/2 teaspoon	2.5 grams
Trisodium phosphate	1/2 teaspoon	2.5 grams
Diatomaceous earth	1 cup	240.0 grams

SKI WAX

Wood tar	1 3/4 cup	420.0 ml
Diglycol stearate	1/2 cup	120.0 grams
Carnauba wax	1/4 cup	60.0 grams

SNOW AND ICE MELTING COMPOUND

Rock salt	4 cups	960.0 grams
Ammonium chloride	8 cups	1.9 kg
Magnesium sulfate	4 cups	960.0 grams

SOOTHING EYEWASH

Sodium bicarbonate	1/16 teaspoon	0.3 gram
Distilled water	1 cup	240.0 ml

146

Formula Ingredients and Their Metric Equivalents

SOOTHING FOOT BATH

Menthol crystals	1/8 teaspoon	0.6 grams
Powdered alum	4 tablespoons	60.0 grams
Boric acid	8 tablespoons	120.0 grams
Magnesium sulfate	10 tablespoons	150.0 grams

SUNTAN LOTION

Isopropyl alcohol	5 tablespoons	75.0 ml
Glycerin	2 tablespoons	30.0 ml
Water	2 cups	480.0 ml
Food coloring	to suit	
Perfume (type 2)	to suit	

SWEDISH FORMULA MOUTHWASH

Borax	1/16 teaspoon	0.3 grams
Boric acid	1 1/2 teaspoons	7.5 grams
Tincture of cloves	to suit	
Water	4 cups	960.0 ml
Food coloring	to suit	

TERMITE PROOFING

Paradichloro-benzene	1 cup	240.0 grams
Denatured alcohol	8 cups	1.9 liters

TILE AND HOUSEHOLD CLEANER

Trisodium phosphate	2 tablespoons	30.0 grams
Water	2 quarts	2.0 liters

Appendix A

TOILET BOWL CLEANER

Sodium bicarbonate	4 cups	960.0 grams
Caustic soda	3/4 cup	180.0 grams

TOOL RUST REMOVER

Ammonium citrate	1 tablespoon	15.0 grams
Water	2 cups	480.0 ml

TOOTHPASTE

Ground pumice	1/2 cup	120.0 grams
Glycerin	1/4 cup	60.0 ml

TYPE CLEANER

Denatured alcohol	1 1/2 cups	360.0 ml
Water	1 cup	240.0 ml

UPHOLSTERY CLEANER

Oil soap	4 tablespoons	60.0 ml
Borax	1 tablespoon	15.0 grams
Glycerin	4 tablespoons	60.0 ml
Ethylene chloride	2 tablespoons	30.0 ml
Hot water	3 quarts	3.0 liters

VINYL CLEANER

Calcium carbonate	1 cup	240.0 grams
Bicarbonate of soda	3 cups	720.0 grams

Formula Ingredients and Their Metric Equivalents

WALL AND WOODWORK CLEANER

Corn flour	4 ounces	120.0 grams
Copper sulfate	1/2 ounce	15.0 grams
Alum	1/8 teaspoon	0.6 grams
Hot water	1 quart	1.0 liter

WATERLESS HAND SOAP

Powdered white soap	1/2 cup	120.0 grams
Potassium carbonate	1/8 cup	30.0 grams
Trisodium phosphate	2 teaspoons	10.0 ml
Powdered asbestos	1/2 cup	120.0 grams
Water	5 cups	1.2 liters
Lemon oil	to suit	

WATERPROOFING CANVAS

Soybean oil	3 cups	700.0 ml
Turpentine	1 1/2 cups	350.0 ml

WATERPROOFING CONCRETE

Ammonium stearate	1 1/4 pounds	600.0 grams
Water	4 gallons	15.0 liters

WATERPROOFING LEATHER

Silicone oil	1 tablespoon	15.0 ml
Stoddard solvent	1 cup	240.0 ml

Appendix A

WATER SOFTENER FOR DISHES AND LAUNDRY

Sodium metaphosphate	1 cup	240.0 grams
Sodium metasilicate	1 cup	240.0 grams
Trisodium phosphate	1/2 cup	120.0 grams

WHIPPED CREAM IMPROVER

Gelatin	1 teaspoon	5.0 grams
Sugar	2 tablespoons	30.0 grams
Chilled cream	1 cup	240.0 ml
Vanilla	to suit	

WHITEWASH

Salt	2 pounds	1.0 kg
Water	1 gallon	4.0 liters
Hydrated lime	7 pounds	3.5 kg

WIG AND HAIRPIECE CLEANER

Talc	1 cup	240.0 grams
Zinc oxide	1 tablespoon	15.0 grams
Calcium carbonate	2 tablespoons	30.0 grams
Boric acid	1 teaspoon	5.0 grams

WOOD FLOOR BLEACH

Sodium metasilicate	9 cups	2.0 kg
Sodium perborate	1 cup	240.0 grams

Formula Ingredients and Their Metric Equivalents

WOOD FLOOR CLEANER

Mineral oil	2 1/4 cups	540.0 ml
Oleic acid	3/4 cup	180.0 ml
Ammonia	2 tablespoons	30.0 ml
Turpentine	5 tablespoons	75.0 ml

WOOD FLOOR LIQUID WAX I

Paraffin	1/8 cup	30.0 grams
Mineral oil	1 quart	1.0 liters

WOOD FLOOR LIQUID WAX II

Yellow beeswax	2 tablespoons	30.0 grams
Ceresin wax	1/2 cup	120.0 grams
Turpentine	2 1/8 cups	500.0 ml
Pine oil	1 tablespoon	15.0 ml

WOOD FLOOR NONSLIP WAX

Orange shellac	1/2 cup	120.0 ml
Acacia	2 tablespoons	30.0 grams
Turpentine	2 tablespoons	30.0 ml
Denatured alcohol	2 cups	480.0 ml

WOOD FLOOR PASTE WAX

Yellow beeswax	2 tablespoons	30.0 grams
Ceresin wax	5 tablespoons	75.0 grams
Carnauba wax	9 tablespoons	135.0 grams
Montan wax	3 tablespoons	45.0 grams
Mineral spirits	1 pint	480.0 ml
Turpentine	4 tablespoons	60.0 ml
Pine oil	1 tablespoon	15.0 ml

Appendix A

WOUND DRESSING FOR TREES AND SHRUBS

Zinc oxide	1 cup	240.0 grams
Mineral oil	2 cups	480.0 ml

WRINKLE LOTION FOR SKIN

Alum	1/4 teaspoon	1.25 grams
Zinc sulfate	1 speck	.3 grams
Glycerin	2 teaspoons	10.0 ml
Tincture of benzoin	2 teaspoons	10.0 ml
Perfume	to suit	
Distilled water	1 quart	1.0 liter

The Four Categories of Formulas Found in *The Formula Book*

$$\text{H-C--C-H with H atoms}$$

1. Dry materials that are simply mixed together. Example:
Drain Cleaner
Mix baking soda, salt, and cream of tartar. These are all simply mixed together.

2. Dry or semisolid materials that become liquids when combined with a solvent such as water or alcohol. Example:
Underarm Deodorant
Dissolve powdered alum (aluminum potassium sulfate) in water and add perfume to suit. In this type of product we have put a dry powder into a solution in a solvent, and our end product becomes a liquid.

3. Materials that require heat to turn them from a solid or semisolid into a liquid and back into a solid on cooling. Example:
Cold Cream
Measure white mineral oil and white beeswax into top section of double boiler. Heat until mass becomes a liquid. Cool down, and at 120° F. stir in perfume and pour into jars. Allow to cool. In this type of compound we have converted a solid and semisolid into a liquid by melting it, and returned it to a semisolid by cooling.

4. Emulsions. Example:
   Polishing Liquid
   Mix silicone oil emulsion concentrate into water. As we all
   know, water and oil will not mix unless the oil is combined
   with an emulsifying agent.

APPENDIX C

Conversion Equivalents

$$\begin{array}{c} H \\ | \\ H-C \\ | \\ H \end{array} \begin{array}{c} H \\ | \\ C-H \\ | \\ H \end{array}$$

3 teaspoons	equals	1 tablespoon
2 tablespoons	equals	1 liquid ounce
4 tablespoons	equals	1/4 cup
16 tablespoons	equals	1 cup
2 cups	equals	1 pint
2 pints	equals	1 quart
4 quarts	equals	1 gallon
16 ounces	equals	1 pound

METRIC CONVERSIONS

We are approaching the time when the metric system will phase out our conventional system of weights and measures. But this is a confusing transition to make, so many people are wisely beginning to learn it now. To aid in their effort, the following tables are included, and the proportions listed in each formula are expressed in both systems. Thus, by association, learning the equivalents is far easier. For simplification of measurement the metric has been rounded out to 1 decimal and specific gravity average. See Appendix A for metric equivalents of the formulas in this book.

Appendix C

CONVERSION FORMULAS

Gallons into Pounds—Multiply 8.33 (wt. 1 gallon of water) by the specific gravity (sg) and the result by the number of gallons. (See any chemical dictionary for the sg of a particular chemical.)

Pounds into Gallons—Multiply 8.33 by the sg and divide the number of pounds by the result.

Milliliters into Grams—Multiply the number of milliliters by the sg.

Grams into Milliliters—Divide the number of grams by the sg.

Milliliters into Pounds—Multiply the number of milliliters by the sg, and divide the product by 453.56 (no. of g. per lb.).

Pounds into Milliliters—Multiply the number of pounds by 453.56 and divide the product by the sg.

Milliliters into Ounces—Multiply the number of milliliters by the sg, and divide the product by 28.35 (no. g. per oz.).

Ounces into Milliliters—Multiply the number of ounces by 28.35 and divide the product by the sg.

CONVERSION FACTORS

Liquid

From	To	Multiply By
Ounces	Milliliters	29.56
Pints	Liters	0.47
Quarts	Liters	0.95
Gallons	Liters	3.78
Milliliters	Ounces	0.03
Liters	Pints	2.10
Liters	Quarts	1.05
Liters	Gallons	0.26

Conversion Equivalents

Dry

From	To	Multiply By
Ounces	Grams	28.35
Pounds	Kilograms	0.45
Grams	Ounces	0.035
Kilograms	Pounds	2.21

FLUID MEASURE

Metric	U.S. Regular
1 milliliter	0.034 ounce
1 liter	33.81 ounces
1 liter	2.10 pints
1 liter	1.05 quarts
1 liter	0.26 gallons

DRY MEASURE

Metric	U.S. Regular
1 gram	0.035 ounce
1 kilogram	35.27 ounces
1 kilogram	2.21 pounds

DRY MEASURE

U.S. Regular	Metric Equivalent
1/8 teaspoon	0.54 grams
1/4 "	1.09 "

Appendix C

U.S. Regular	Metric Equivalent
1/2 teaspoon	2.19 grams
3/4 "	3.28 "
1 "	4.38 "
1/8 tablespoon	1.77 grams
1/4 "	3.54 "
1/2 "	7.09 "
3/4 "	10.63 "
1 "	14.18 "
1/8 ounce	3.59 grams
1/4 "	7.39 "
1/2 "	14.18 "
3/4 "	21.34 "
1 "	28.35 "
1/8 pound	56.69 grams
1/4 "	113.39 "
1/2 "	226.78 "
3/4 "	340.17 "
1 "	453.56 "
1/8 cup	28.34 grams
1/4 "	56.69 "
1/2 "	113.39 "
3/4 "	170.08 "
1 "	226.78 "

LIQUID MEASURE

U.S. Regular	Metric Equivalent
1/8 teaspoon	0.61 milliliters
1/4 "	1.23 "
1/2 "	2.47 "
3/4 "	3.70 "
1 "	4.94 "

Conversion Equivalents

U.S. Regular	Metric Equivalent
1/8 tablespoon	1.84 milliliters
1/4 "	3.69 "
1/2 "	7.39 "
3/4 "	11.08 "
1 "	14.78 "
1/8 ounce	3.69 milliliters
1/4 "	7.39 "
1/2 "	14.78 "
3/4 "	22.17 "
1 "	29.57 "
1/8 cup	29.57 milliliters
1/4 "	59.14 "
1/2 "	118.28 "
3/4 "	177.42 "
1 "	236.56 "
1 pint	473.00 milliliters
1 quart	946.00 "
1/2 gallon	1.89 liters
3/4 "	2.83 "
1 "	3.78 "

APPENDIX 4

Temperature Conversion Tables

NOTE: -- The numbers in bold face type refer to the temperature either in degrees Centigrade or Fahrenheit which is to be converted into the other scale. If converting from Fahrenheit to Centigrade the equivalent temperature will be found in the left column. When converting from degrees Centigrade to Fahrenheit, the answer will be found in the column on the right. Interpolation factors are at the bottom right hand corner of the table.

C.		F.
-17.8	0	32
-17.2	1	33.8
-16.7	2	35.6
-16.1	3	37.4
-15.6	4	39.2
-15.0	5	41.0
-14.4	6	42.8
-13.9	7	44.6
-13.3	8	46.4
-12.8	9	48.2
-12.2	10	50.0
-11.7	11	51.8
-11.1	12	53.6
-10.6	13	55.4
-10.0	14	57.2
-9.44	15	59.0
-8.89	16	60.8
-8.33	17	62.6
-7.78	18	64.4
-7.22	19	66.2
-6.67	20	68.0
-6.11	21	69.8
-5.56	22	71.6
-5.00	23	73.4
-4.44	24	75.2
-3.89	25	77.0
-3.33	26	78.8
-2.78	27	80.6
-2.22	28	82.4
-1.67	29	84.2
-1.11	30	86.0
-0.56	31	87.8
0	32	89.6
0.56	33	91.4
1.11	34	93.2
1.67	35	95.0
2.22	36	96.8
2.78	37	98.6
3.33	38	100.4
3.89	39	102.2
4.44	40	104.0
5.00	41	105.8
5.56	42	107.6
6.11	43	109.4
6.67	44	111.2
7.22	45	113.0
7.78	46	114.8
8.33	47	116.6
8.89	48	118.4
9.44	49	120.2

C.		F.
10.0	50	122.0
10.6	51	123.8
11.1	52	125.6
11.7	53	127.4
12.2	54	129.2
12.8	55	131.0
13.3	56	132.8
13.9	57	134.6
14.4	58	136.4
15.0	59	138.2
15.6	60	140.0
16.1	61	141.8
16.7	62	143.6
17.2	63	145.4
17.8	64	147.2
18.3	65	149.0
18.9	66	150.8
19.4	67	152.6
20.0	68	154.4
20.6	69	156.2
21.1	70	158.0
21.7	71	159.8
22.2	72	161.6
22.8	73	163.4
23.3	74	165.2
23.9	75	167.0
24.4	76	168.8
25.0	77	170.6
25.6	78	172.4
26.1	79	174.2
26.7	80	176.0
27.2	81	177.8
27.8	82	179.6
28.3	83	181.4
28.9	84	183.2
29.4	85	185.0
30.0	86	186.8
30.6	87	188.6
31.1	88	190.4
31.7	89	192.2
32.2	90	194.0
32.8	91	195.8
33.3	92	197.6
33.9	93	199.4
34.4	94	201.2
35.0	95	203.0
35.6	96	204.8
36.1	97	206.6
36.7	98	208.4
37.2	99	210.2

C.		F.
38	100	212
43	110	230
49	120	248
54	130	266
60	140	284
66	150	302
71	160	320
77	170	338
82	180	356
88	190	374
93	200	392
99	210	410
104	220	428
110	230	446
116	240	464
121	250	482
127	260	500
132	270	518
138	280	536
143	290	554
149	300	572
154	310	590
160	320	608
166	330	626
171	340	644
177	350	662
182	360	680
188	370	698
193	380	716
199	390	734
204	400	752
210	410	770
216	420	788
221	430	806
227	440	824
232	450	842
238	460	860
243	470	878
249	480	896
254	490	914
260	500	932
266	510	950
271	520	968
277	530	986
282	540	1004
288	550	1022
293	560	1040
299	570	1058
304	580	1076
310	590	1094

C.		F.
316	600	1112
321	610	1130
327	620	1148
332	630	1166
338	640	1184
343	650	1202
349	660	1220
354	670	1238
360	680	1256
366	690	1274
371	700	1292
377	710	1310
382	720	1328
388	730	1346
393	740	1364
399	750	1382
404	760	1400
410	770	1418
416	780	1436
421	790	1454
427	800	1472
432	810	1490
438	820	1508
443	830	1526
449	840	1544
454	850	1562
460	860	1580
466	870	1598
471	880	1616
477	890	1634
482	900	1652
488	910	1670
493	920	1688
499	930	1706
504	940	1724
510	950	1742
516	960	1760
521	970	1778
527	980	1796
532	990	1814
538	1000	1832
543	1010	1850
549	1020	1868
554	1030	1886
560	1040	1904
566	1050	1922
571	1060	1940
577	1070	1958
582	1080	1976
588	1090	1994

C.		F.
593	1100	2012
599	1110	2030
604	1120	2048
610	1130	2066
616	1140	2084
621	1150	2102
627	1160	2120
632	1170	2138
638	1180	2156
643	1190	2174
649	1200	2192
654	1210	2210
660	1220	2228
666	1230	2246
671	1240	2264
677	1250	2282
682	1260	2300
688	1270	2318
693	1280	2336
699	1290	2354
704	1300	2372
710	1310	2390
716	1320	2408
721	1330	2426
727	1340	2444
732	1350	2462
738	1360	2480
743	1370	2498
749	1380	2516
754	1390	2534
760	1400	2552
766	1410	2570
771	1420	2588
777	1430	2606
782	1440	2624
788	1450	2642
793	1460	2660
799	1470	2678
804	1480	2696
810	1490	2714
816	1500	2732
821	1510	2750
827	1520	2768
832	1530	2786
838	1540	2804
843	1550	2822
849	1560	2840
854	1570	2858
860	1580	2876
866	1590	2894

C.		F.
871	1600	2912
877	1610	2930
882	1620	2948
888	1630	2966
893	1640	2984
899	1650	3002
904	1660	3020
910	1670	3038
916	1680	3056
921	1690	3074
927	1700	3092
932	1710	3110
938	1720	3128
943	1730	3146
949	1740	3164
954	1750	3182
960	1760	3200
966	1770	3218
971	1780	3236
977	1790	3254
982	1800	3272
988	1810	3290
993	1820	3308
999	1830	3326
1004	1840	3344
1010	1850	3362
1016	1860	3380
1021	1870	3398
1027	1880	3416
1032	1890	3434
1038	1900	3452
1043	1910	3470
1049	1920	3488
1054	1930	3506
1060	1940	3524
1066	1950	3542
1071	1960	3560
1077	1970	3578
1082	1980	3596
1088	1990	3614
1093	2000	3632
1099	2010	3650
1104	2020	3668
1110	2030	3686
1116	2040	3704
1121	2050	3722
1127	2060	3740
1132	2070	3758
1138	2080	3776
1143	2090	3794

C.		F.
1149	2100	3812
1154	2110	3830
1160	2120	3848
1166	2130	3866
1171	2140	3884
1177	2150	3902
1182	2160	3920
1188	2170	3938
1193	2180	3956
1199	2190	3974
1204	2200	3992
1210	2210	4010
1216	2220	4028
1221	2230	4046
1227	2240	4064
1232	2250	4082
1238	2260	4100
1243	2270	4118
1249	2280	4136
1254	2290	4154
1260	2300	4172
1266	2310	4190
1271	2320	4208
1277	2330	4226
1282	2340	4244
1288	2350	4262
1293	2360	4280
1299	2370	4298
1304	2380	4316
1310	2390	4334
1316	2400	4352
1321	2410	4370
1327	2420	4388
1332	2430	4406
1338	2440	4424
1343	2450	4442
1349	2460	4460
1354	2470	4478
1360	2480	4496
1366	2490	4514
1371	2500	4532
1377	2510	4550
1382	2520	4568
1388	2530	4586
1393	2540	4604
1399	2550	4622
1404	2560	4640
1410	2570	4658
1416	2580	4676
1421	2590	4694

C.		F.
1427	2600	4712
1432	2610	4730
1438	2620	4748
1443	2630	4766
1449	2640	4784
1454	2650	4802
1460	2660	4820
1466	2670	4838
1471	2680	4856
1477	2690	4874
1482	2700	4892
1488	2710	4910
1493	2720	4928
1499	2730	4946
1504	2740	4964
1510	2750	4982
1516	2760	5000
1521	2770	5018
1527	2780	5036
1532	2790	5054
1538	2800	5072
1543	2810	5090
1549	2820	5108
1554	2830	5126
1560	2840	5144
1566	2850	5162
1571	2860	5180
1577	2870	5198
1582	2880	5216
1588	2890	5234
1593	2900	5252
1599	2910	5270
1604	2920	5288
1610	2930	5306
1616	2940	5324
1621	2950	5342
1627	2960	5360
1632	2970	5378
1638	2980	5396
1643	2990	5414
1649	3000	5432

INTERPOLATION FACTORS

0.56	1	1.8
1.11	2	3.6
1.67	3	5.4
2.22	4	7.2
2.78	5	9.0
3.33	6	10.8
3.89	7	12.6
4.44	8	14.4
5.00	9	16.2
5.56	10	18.0

APPENDIX E

Sources of Chemicals

$$H-\overset{H}{\underset{H}{C}}---\overset{H}{\underset{H}{C}}-H$$

Below is a list of ingredients and sources of supply used in The Formula Book, followed by the number of times these ingredients are used, for the convenience of the consumer who must buy these ingredients in small quantities.

acacia (gum arabic): drugstore or chemical supply house, 3
activated charcoal: drugstore, 1
almond oil: paint or hardware store, 2
alum: drugstore, 14
aluminum powder: paint or hardware store, 2
aluminum stearate: paint store or chemical supply house, 1
ammonium carbonate: drugstore or chemical supply house, 1
ammonium chloride: drugstore or chemical supply house, 1
ammonium citrate: drugstore or chemical supply house, 1
ammonium hydroxide: drugstore or chemical supply house, 1
ammonium oleate: drugstore or chemical supply house, 1
ammonium phosphate, garden supply store, 2
ammonium selenate: drugstore or chemical supply house, 1
ammonium stearate: drugstore or chemical supply house, 1
ammonium sulfate: garden supply house, 5
amyl acetate: drugstore or chemical supply house, 2
anhydrous lanolin: drugstore or chemical supply house, 2
anthracene: Ward's (see address below), 1
antimony chloride: drugstore or chemical supply house, 2
asbestos: hardware store, 3
asphalt: building material dealer, 1
beeswax: hobby store, 12

Appendix E

benzene: chemical supply or solvent dealer, 3
benzoic acid: drugstore or chemical supply house, 1
bergamot oil: drugstore or chemical supply house, 1
borax: grocery or hardware store, 10
boric acid: drugstore, 12
bran oil: feed and grain store, 1
brown sugar: grocery store, 1
calcium carbonate: drugstore, chemical supply house, feed and grain store or
    building material dealer, 6
calcium chloride: drugstore or county and state highway departments, 3
camphor: drugstore, 2
carnauba wax: hobby shop, 5
Castile soap: drugstore, 1
castor oil: drugstore or chemical supply house, 6
caustic potash (lye): grocery store, 4
caustic soda (lye): grocery store, 8
cement: building supply, 1
ceresin wax: hobby shop, 4
chalk (calcium carbonate): drugstore or chemical supply house, 6
chlorinated lime: building supply, 1
cinnamon oil: drugstore or chemical supply house, 1
citric acid: drugstore or chemical supply house, 2
citronella oil: drugstore or chemical supply house, 1
cocoa powder: grocery store, 1
coconut oil: chemical supply house, 2
copper naphthenate: chemical supply dealer, 2
copper sulfate: drugstore or chemical supply house, 2
corn flour: grocery store, 1
corn oil: grocery store or chemical supply house, 1
cornstarch: grocery store, 3
corn syrup: grocery store, 1
cream of tartar: grocery store, 1
creosote: hardware, paint or building supply, 1
cresylic acid: drugstore or chemical supply house, 1
denatured alcohol: drugstore or chemical supply house, 37
diatomaceous earth: swimming pool supply dealer, 2
diglycol laurate: drugstore or chemical supply house, 1
diglycol stearate: drugstore or chemical supply house, 1

162

dimethylmorpholine: chemical supply house, 1

dried yeast: grocery store, 1

dye: drugstore or hardware store, 3

ethyl alcohol (vodka): liquor store, 1

ethylene chloride: drugstore or chemical supply house, 1

ethylene glycol (antifreeze): automotive store or hardware store, 2

eucalyptus oil: drugstore, 1

ferric chloride: chemical supply house, 2

flour: grocery store, 1

fuel or auto drain oil: automotive store or oil distributors, 4

Fuller's earth: ceramic supply stores or building material dealer, 2

furfuraldehyde: drugstore or chemical supply house, oil distributors, 1

gelatin: grocery store, 3

glycerin: drugstore, 23

gum rosin: music store (used for violin bows), 1

honey: grocery store, 1

household ammonia: grocery store, 7

hydrated lime: drugstore, feed and grain store, oil distributor, or chemical supply house, 2

hydrogen peroxide: drugstore, 2

iron oxide: chemical supply house, 1

isopropyl alcohol: drugstore or solvent distributor (may be substituted for denatured alcohol), 9

kerosene: paint or hardware store, oil distributor, 11

lactic acid: drugstore, 1

lanolin: drugstore or chemical supply house, 2

lauryl pyridinium chloride: chemical supply house, 3

lead (powdered): chemical supply house or building material dealer, 1

lemon oil: drugstore, 7

linseed oil: hardware or paint store, 2

liquid latex: hobby shop or ceramic supply store, 1

magnesium sulfate (epsom salts): drugstore, 2

mason sand: building material dealer, 1

menthol: drugstore, 1

mercuric chloride: chemical supply house, 1

methyl salicylate: drugstore or chemical supply house, 1

mineral oil: drugstore or chemical supply house, 24

mineral spirits: solvent dealer, 1

molasses: grocery store, 1

montan wax: drugstore or chemical supply house, 2

naphtha: oil distributor or chemical supply house, 2

naphthalene: drugstore or chemical supply house, 1

neat's-foot oil: boot and shoe store, 2

neroli oil: drugstore, 1

oil soap (see Castile soap)

oleic acid: chemical supply house, 5

olive oil: grocery store, 1

orange shellac: paint or hardware store, 1

oxalic acid: chemical supply dealer, 1

oxyquinoline sulfate: drugstore or chemical supply house, 1

parachlorometacresol: drugstore or chemical supply house, 1

paradichlorobenzene (moth crystals): hardware store, 2

paraffin oil: oil distributor, 3

paraffin wax: grocery store or hobby shop, 8

peanut oil: grocery store, 1

peppermint oil: drugstore, 2

petrolatum: drugstore, oil distributor or chemical supply house, 6

petroleum distillate: oil distributor or chemical supply house, 1

pine oil: hardware store, 5

potassium carbonate (potash): chemical supply house, 4

potassium nitrate: drugstore or chemical supply house, 1

potassium oleate: chemical supply house, 1

potassium persulfate: chemical supply house, 1

propylene glycol: chemical supply house, 1

pumice: hardware store, 2

pyrethrin: garden supply store, 3

rape seed oil: drugstore or chemical supply house, 1

rock salt: grocery store or water softener dealer, 3

rosemary oil: drugstore or chemical supply house, 1

rosin: music store or athletic supply store, 1

rottenstone powder: hardware or paint store, 1

salicylic acid: drugstore or pharmaceutical dealer, 2

sand: building material dealer, 1

sawdust: lumberyard, 3

sesame oil: grocery store, 1

silica gel: refrigeration service, 1

silicone liquid emulsion: chemical supply house or foundry supply, 2
silicone oil: foundry or foundry supply dealer, 3
silver nitrate: drugstore, 1
soda ash: hardware store, swimming pool supplier, 6
sodium alginate: drugstore or chemical supply house, 1
sodium aluminate: chemical supply house, 1
sodium bicarbonate (baking soda): grocery store, 12
sodium bisulfite: chemical supply house, 1
sodium carbonate: drugstore or chemical supply house, 2
sodium chloride (salt): grocery store or feed and grain supply house, 4
sodium dodecylbenzene sulfate: drugstore or chemical supply house, 1
sodium lauryl sulfate: drugstore or chemical supply house, 1
sodium metaphosphate: laundry supply dealer, 1
sodium metasilicate: laundry supply dealer, 6
sodium pentachlorophenate: drugstore or chemical supply house, 1
sodium perborate: drugstore, 5
sodium phosphate: drugstore or chemical supply house, 1
sodium sesquicarbonate: drugstore or chemical supply house, 1
sodium silicate (waterglass): drugstore or foundry supply dealers, 5
sodium sulfate: drugstore or pharmaceutical dealers, 2
sodium sulfite: photographic supply store, 2
sodium thiosulfate: photographic supply store, 1
sodium tripolyphosphate: drugstore or chemical supply house, 1
soybean oil: grocery or health food stores, 1
stearamide: drugstore or chemical supply house, 1
stearic acid: hobby shops, 7
Stoddard solvent: solvent dealer or dry cleaning supply dealers, 3
sugar: grocery store, 3
sulfite liquor: county highway department, 1
sulfonated castor oil: drugstore, 1
superphosphate: feed and grain supply house or chemical supply house, 1
talc: drugstore, 7
tallow: meat market, 1
tannic acid: drugstore or chemical supply house, 1
tartaric acid: drugstore or chemical supply house, 1
tin, (powdered): sheet metal shops, 1
tincture of benzoin: drugstore, 2
tincture of rhubarb: drugstore, 1

Appendix E

titanium dioxide: ceramic shop, 1

tragacanth: drugstore or chemical supply house, 2

trichloroethylene: drugstore, chemical supply house, paint or hardware stores, 1

triethanolamine: drugstore or chemical supply house, 7

trisodium phosphate: hardware store, 13

turpentine: hardware and paint store, 12

ultramarine blue: drugstore or paint store, 1

vanilla: grocery store, 1

vermiculite: building supply dealer, 1

vinegar: grocery store, 1

wheat starch: grocery store, 1

white petrolatum: drugstore, 1

whiting: (See *chalk*)

whole-wheat flour: grocery store, 1

witch hazel: drugstore, 2

wood tar: drugstore or chemical supply house, 1

yellow dextrin: drugstore or chemical supply house, 1

zinc bromide: photographic supply store, 1

zinc chloride: feed and grain dealer, 3

zinc oxide: ceramic shop or drugstore, 4

zinc powder: electroplating supply dealer, 2

zinc sulfate: drugstore or chemical supply dealer, 1

Specialized Sources of Chemicals

$$H-\underset{H}{\overset{H}{C}}\text{———}\underset{H}{\overset{H}{C}}-H$$

1. *Repackagers of Chemicals.* We have located the following.

Ward's Natural Science Establishment, Inc., P.O. Box 1712, Rochester, New York 14603, or P.O. 1749, Monterey, Calif. 93940.

This reliable old company publishes a beautiful catalog which the writer has before him. Beginning on page 116 is a listing of well over 1000 chemicals that are available in small quantities by mail. Almost anything that could possibly be needed will be found here. However, the more common chemicals found at local sources will be lower in cost.

*Drake Bros. Chemical Company, N. 57, W. 13636, Menomonee Falls, Wisconsin
*Fischer Scientific Company, 711 Forbes Ave., Pittsburgh, Pennsylvania
*Berg Chemical Company, 441 N. 37th Street, New York, N.Y.

*At the time of writing catalogs have not been received.

2. *Manufacturers:* Many chemical manufacturers have local offices in principal cities. Frequently they are listed under the product you wish to locate. For example, under Silicones in the Yellow Pages may be found Dow Corning, or Union Carbide. All principal manufacturers are listed, under the product you seek, in the O.P.D. Chemical Buyers Directory, Schnell Publishing Company. Most libraries will have a copy.

APPENDIX F

Definitions of Chemicals Used in *The Formula Book*

$$\text{H}-\underset{\underset{\displaystyle \text{H}}{|}}{\overset{\overset{\displaystyle \text{H}}{\diagdown}}{\text{C}}}-\underset{\underset{\displaystyle \text{H}}{|}}{\overset{\overset{\displaystyle \text{H}}{\diagup}}{\text{C}}}-\text{H}$$

ACACIA (gum arabic): White powder or flakes, soluble in water. Dried from the plant *Acacia Senegal.*

ACTIVATED CHARCOAL: Black powder. Obtained by the destructive distillation of carbonaceous materials such as wood or nut shells. It is activated by heating to approximately 900° C. with steam or carbon dioxide which produces a honeycomb internal structure, making it highly adsorptive.

ALMOND OIL: White to yellowish oil, distilled from ground kernels of bitter almonds imported from Spain, Portugal or France. Caution: Vapors are toxic.

ALUMINUM POTASSIUM SULFATE (alum): White crystals or powder, soluble in water. Derived from alunite leucite and other minerals. Acts as an astringent.

ALUMINUM POWDER: Gray to silver powder, milled from aluminum or its alloys. Particles are dispersed in a vehicle such as paint.

ALUMINUM STEARATE: White powder, soluble in petroleum and turpentine oil. Made by reacting aluminum salts with stearic acid.

AMMONIA, HOUSEHOLD: A dilute solution of ammonium hydroxide. Caution: Do not breathe vapors, avoid contact with skin.

168

AMMONIA SELENATE: Colorless crystals, soluble in water. Caution: May be mildly toxic.

AMMONIUM CARBONATE (hartshorn): White powder, soluble in cold water. A mixture of ammonium acid carbonate and ammonium carbamate. Derived from the heating of ammonium salts with calcium carbonate. Caution: When heated, irritating fumes may result.

AMMONIUM CHLORIDE (sal ammoniac): White crystals, soluble in water and glycerol. Derived from the reaction of ammonium sulfate and sodium chloride solutions.

AMMONIUM CITRATE: White granules, soluble in water.

AMMONIUM HYDROXIDE (aqua ammonium): Water solution of ammonia gas. Caution: Toxic by ingestion. Liquid and vapors may be irritating to eyes and skin.

AMMONIUM OLEATE (ammonia soap): Brown jellylike mass, soluble in water and alcohol. Acts as an emulsifying agent.

AMMONIUM NITRATE (saltpeter): Colorless crystals, soluble in water, alcohol and alkalies. Made by the action of ammonia vapor on nitric acid. Caution: Do not store in high temperatures.

AMMONIUM PHOSPHATE: White crystals moderately soluble in water. Derived from the interaction of phosphoric acid and ammonia.

AMMONIUM STEARATE: Tan waxlike solid, dispersable in hot water, soluble in hot toluene.

AMMONIUM SULFATE: Gray to white crystals, soluble in water. Made by neutralizing synthetic ammonia with sulfuric acid.

AMYL ACETATE (banana oil): Volatile banana like smell. Caution: Flammable, fire risk, moderately toxic by inhalation and ingestion.

ANHYDROUS LANOLIN (wool fat): Brown jelly, miscible with water. Soluble in benzene, ether, acetone and slightly soluble in cold alcohol.

Appendix F

ANTHRACENE OIL: A coal tar fraction. Hazard, toxic and irritant.

ANTIMONY CHLORIDE: White powder soluble in hydrochloric acid and alkali tartrate solutions. Caution: Highly toxic.

ASBESTOS POWDER: Gray fiberous powder. Mined as a natural mineral. Caution: Do not inhale dust.

ASPHALT (residual oil, petroleum asphalt, trinidad pitch, mineral pitch): Solid to semisolid lumps, turns to viscous liquid at 200°F.

BENZENE: Colorless liquid, made by the catalytic reforming of petroleum, and also by the fractional distillation of coal tar. Caution: Highly flammable and toxic by prolonged inhalation.

BENZOIC ACID (carboxybenzene): White scales or needlelike crystals, soluble in alcohol, ether, chloroform, benzene and turpentine. Made by the oxidation of toluene. Caution: May cause nausea if taken internally in concentrated form.

BERGAMOT OIL: Honey colored oil, soluble in alcohol. Derived from the fruits of *Citrus Bergamia Risso et Painteau*.

BORAX (sodium borate): White powder, soluble in water. Mined in the western United States.

BORIC ACID (boracic acid): Colorless odorless white powder, soluble in water, alcohol and glycerin. Made by the addition of hydrochloric or sulfuric acid to a borax solution, and then crystallizing.

CALCIUM CARBONATE (chalk): White powder, slightly soluble in water, highly soluble in acids. Derived principally from limestone.

CALCIUM CHLORIDE: White flakes that decompose in water. Absorptive agent.

CAMPHOR (gum camphor, camphanone): Colorless or white crystals, soluble in alcohol. Derivation: steam distillation of camphor tree wood. Vapors flammable.

CAMPHOR OIL: Pale yellow oily liquid. Derivation: steam distillation of camphor tree wood and separation of oil. Flammable.

CARNAUBA WAX (Brazil wax): Yellow to brown hard lumps, melting point 84°-86°C. Collected from the leaves of the Brazilian wax palm, *Copernicia cerifera*.

CASTOR OIL (recinus oil): Pale yellow oil, soluble in alcohol. Derived from pressing the seeds of the castor bean, *Ricinus communis*.

CAUSTIC POTASH (potassium hydroxide): White flakes, soluble in alcohol, water, or glycerin. Made by electrolysis of a potassium chloride solution. Caution: Highly toxic by ingestion, skin irritant.

CAUSTIC SODA (sodium hydroxide): White chips, soluble in water or alcohol. Made by electrolysis of a sodium chloride solution. Caution: Heats on contact with water, can cause severe burns to skin. Handle with care. Store in airtight container.

CERESIN WAX (ozocerite, mineral wax): White or yellow solid, soluble in alcohol. Melting point 68°-72°C. Made by purifying ozocerite with sulfuric acid and then filtering through charcoal.

CHLORINATED LIME (bleaching powder): White granules that decompose in water. Made by reacting chlorine with slaked lime. Caution: Forms chlorine when mixed into water. Do not breathe vapors or allow skin and clothes contact.

CINNAMON OIL (cassia oil): Light yellow aromatic oil, soluble in alcohol. Distilled from the leaves and twigs of the plant *Cinnamomum Cassia*.

CITRIC ACID: White crystals, soluble in water or alcohol. Derived by mold fermentation from lemon, lime, pineapple juice, and molasses.

CITRONELLA OIL: Light yellow essential oil, soluble in alcohol. Derived by the steam distillation of the grass of *Cymbopogon Nardus*. Caution: Mildly toxic if taken internally.

COCONUT OIL: White, semisolid lardlike fat. Soluble in alcohol. Melting point, 83°F. Made by press extraction of coconut meat followed by alkali refining.

COPPER NAPHTHENATE: A green-blue solid, soluble in gasoline, benzene and mineral oil distillates. Made by combining cupric to a solution of sodium naphthenate. Caution: Mildly toxic by ingestion.

COPPER SULFATE (blue vitreol, bluestone): Blue crystals, lumps, or powder. Soluble in water or methanol. Made by the action of dilute sulfuric acid on copper or its oxides. Caution: Highly toxic by ingestion.

CORN OIL (maize oil): Pale yellow liquid, partially soluble in alcohol. The germ is removed from the kernel and cold pressed.

CORN SYRUP (glucose): Viscous liquid consisting of a mixture of dextrose, maltose, and dextrius with about 20% water. Soluble in water and glycerin. Made by the hydrolysis of starch and the action of hydrochloric acid.

CREOSOTE (wood tar, beechwood): Colorless oily liquid, miscible with alcohol or ether. A mixture of phenols obtained by the destructive distillation of wood tar. Caution: Moderately toxic by ingestion.

CRESYLIC ACID: A commercial mixture of phenolic materials, made from petroleum or coal tar. Caution: Corrosive to skin.

DENATURED ALCOHOL: Ethyl alcohol that has been contaminated with a minute amount of another material to make it unfit for human consumption as a beverage. Clear white liquid. Caution: May be toxic if taken internally. Flammable.

DIATOMACEOUS EARTH (kieselguhr, diatomite): A bulky light material containing 88% silica. The balance is made up of the skeletons of small prehistoric plants related to algae. Can be had in either brick or powdered form.

DIGLYCOL LAURATE (diethylene glycol monolaurate): Straw colored oily liquid, non-toxic. Dispersable in water. Derived from thelauric acid ester of diethylene glycol.

DIGLYCOL STEARATE: White waxlike solid. Disperses in hot water, soluble in hot alcohol. Made by using stearic acid and the ester of diethylene glycol.

DIMETHYLMORPHOLINE: Liquid. Flash point 112°F. Caution: Flammable.

ETHYL ALCOHOL (Vodka): See Appendix G.

ETHYLENE CHLORIDE (ethylene dichloride): Colorless oily liquid, miscible with most organic solvents. Made by the action of chlorine on ethylene. Caution: Toxic by ingestion, inhalation and skin absorption. Irritant to eyes and skin. Handle with care.

ETHYLENE GLYCOL (glycol): Clear colorless syrupy liquid, soluble in water and alcohol. Made from formaldehyde, water, and carbon monoxide with hydrogenation of the resulting glycolic acid.

EUCALYPTUS OIL (eucalyptol): Colorless oil, camphor-like odor and pungent, cooling, spicy taste. Slightly soluble in water, miscible with alcohol. It is moderately toxic.

FERRIC CHLORIDE (iron chloride): A black brown solid, soluble in water, alcohol and glycerol. Made by the action of chlorine on ferrous sulfate.

FUEL OIL (furnace oil): Number 1 or 2 grade. Oil used in home heating furnaces. Caution: Flammable.

FULLER'S EARTH: A porous colloidal aluminum silicate of 1 micron or less, having high adsorptive power. Mined in Florida, England and Canada.

FURFURALDEHYDE (bran oil): Colorless liquid, soluble in water. Derived from grain hulls. Caution: Highly toxic, can be absorbed through skin.

GELATIN: White to yellow powder, soluble in hot water. Made by boiling animal by-products with water. Will absorb up to ten times its weight of water.

GLYCERIN (glycerol): A clear, colorless, syrupy liquid, soluble in water and alcohol. Made by the hydrogenation of carbohydrates with a nickel catalyst.

HYDRATED LIME (calcium hydroxide): White powder, soluble in glycerin. Made by the action of water on calcium oxide.

HYDROGEN PEROXIDE: Colorless dilute aqueous solution. May be further diluted with water. Caution: Highly toxic in concentrated form. Relatively low toxicity in dilute aqueous solution.

IRON OXIDE (jeweler's rouge): Reddish brown fine powder, soluble in acids. Made by the interaction of a solution of ferrous sulfate and sodium carbonate.

KEROSENE: Oily liquid distilled from petroleum. Caution: Toxic if taken internally. Flammable.

LACTIC ACID (milk acid): Colorless viscous liquid, miscible with water, alcohol, and glycerin. Made by the hydrolysis of lactronitrile.

LANOLIN (wool fat): Yellow to light gray semi-solid, soluble in ether or chloroform. Extracted from raw wool and refined.

LATEX (liquid rubber): A white free flowing liquid obtained from certain species of trees and shrubs. Usually emulsified with water.

LAURYL PYRIDINIUM CHLORIDE: Mottled tan semisolid, soluble in water.

LEAD: Heavy soft gray metal solid, soluble in dilute nitric acid. Made by the roasting of lead sulfide, lead sulfate and lead carbonate. Caution: Poison.

LEMON OIL: Yellow liquid, soluble in alcohol, vegetable oils and mineral oil. Expressed from the peel of lemons.

LINSEED OIL: Amber to brown oil, soluble in alcohol. Made by refining raw linseed oil. Warning: Dries when exposed to air. Keep in airtight container.

MAGNESIUM SULFATE (Epsom salts): Colorless crystals, soluble in water and glycerol. Made by the action of sulfuric acid on magnesium oxide.

MENTHOL (peppermint camphor): White crystals with strong mint odor, soluble in alcohol, petroleum solvents and glacial acetic acid. Crystals are formed as a result of freezing mint oil. Caution: Avoid vapors and skin contact in concentrated form.

MERCURIC CHLORIDE: White crystals or powder, soluble in water, alcohol or ether. Caution: Highly toxic by ingestion, inhalation, and skin absorption.

METHYLSALICYLATE (wintergreen oil): Colorless or yellow or reddish liquid, soluble in alcohol and glacial acetic acid. Made by heating methanol and salicylic acid in the presence of sulfuric acid.

MINERAL OIL—WHITE (liquid petrolatum): Colorless transparent oil, distilled from petroleum. Flammable.

MINERAL SPIRITS (petroleum naphtha): Clear liquid, from the petroleum distillation process. Flammable.

MONTAN WAX (lignite wax): White hard earth wax, soluble in benzene. Melting point 90°C. Made by extraction of lignite from coal.

NAPHTHA: White, highly volitile liquid, made in the petroleum distillation process. Caution: Highly flammable.

NAPHTHALENE (tar camphor): White crystalline flakes, soluble in benzene, absolute alcohol and ether. Made by boiling coal tar oil and then crystallizing. Caution: Moderately toxic.

NEAT'S-FOOT OIL: A pale yellow oil, soluble in alcohol and kerosene. Made by boiling, in water, the shinbones and feet, without hoofs, of cattle. The oil and fat are then separated.

NEROLI OIL (orange flower oil): Amber colored oil, soluble in equal parts of alcohol. Made by the distillation of citrus flowers.

Appendix F

OLEIC ACID (red oil): Yellow to red oily liquid, soluble in alcohol and organic solvents. Derived from animal tallow or vegetable oils.

OLIVE OIL: Pale yellow to greenish liquid, non-drying. Only slightly soluble in alcohol. Soluble in ether, chloroform or carbon disulfide. Oil is cold pressed from the olive fruit and then refined.

OXALIC ACID: Transparent colorless crystals, formed in nature by the oxidation of proteins in plants such as wood sorrel, rhubarb and spinach. Caution: Highly toxic by inhalation and ingestion, skin irritant.

OXYQUINOLINE SULFATE: Pale yellow powder, soluble in water. Moderately toxic in concentrated form.

PARADICHLOROBENZENE (moth crystals): White volitile crystals, soluble in alcohol, benzene and ether. Made by chlorination of monochlorobenzene. Moderately toxic by ingestion. Irritant to eyes.

PARAFFIN OIL: An oil that is pressed from paraffin distillate. For characteristics, see paraffin wax. Flammable.

PARAFFIN WAX: White waxy blocks, soluble in benzene, warm alcohol, turpentine and olive oil. Made by distilling crude petroleum oil. Flammable.

PEANUT OIL (groundnut oil): Yellow oil, soluble in petroleum ether, carbon disulfide and chloroform. Can be saponified by alkali hydroxides to form a soap.

PEPPERMINT OIL: Clear oily liquid, soluble in alcohol. Made by distilling the leaves of the peppermint plant.

PETROLATUM (mineral wax, petroleum jelly, mineral jelly): Colorless to amber oily translucent mass, soluble in benzene, ether, chloroform and oil. Melting point, 60°C. Made by the distillation of still residues from steam distillation of paraffin based petroleum. Flammable.

176

PETROLEUM DISTILLATE: Colorless volitile liquid, miscible with most organic solvents and oils. Made by distillation from petroleum. Flammable.

PINE OIL: Colorless to amber oily liquid. Miscible with alcohol. Made by the steam distillation of pine wood.

PORTLAND CEMENT: White to gray powder composed of lime, alumina, silica and iron oxide.

POTASH (potassium carbonate, pearl ash): White deliquescent translucent powder, soluble in water. Caution: Toxic if taken internally.

POTASSIUM CARBONATE: See *potash*.

POTASSIUM NITRATE (niter, saltpeter): Transparent or white crystals or powder, soluble in water. Caution: Dangerous fire and explosion risk when subjected to shock or heating. Oxidizing agent. Handle carefully.

POTASSIUM OLEATE: Gray to tan paste, soluble in water and alcohol.

POTASSIUM PERSULFATE: White crystals, soluble in water. Made by the electrolysis of a saturated solution of potassium sulfate. Hazard: Moderately toxic.

PROPYLENE GLYCOL: Colorless viscous liquid, odorless and tasteless. Miscible with water and alcohol. Made by hydration of propylene oxide.

PUMICE POWDER: A gently abrasive fine powder milled from porous rock found in nature.

PYRETHRIN: A powder obtained from milling ground pyrethrum flowers. Usually mixed with kerosene or other solvents. Caution: Moderately toxic if taken internally.

RAPE SEED OIL (colza oil, rape oil): Pale yellow viscous liquid, soluble in ether, chloroform and carbon disulfide. Made by expression or solvent extraction of rape seeds.

ROSEMARY OIL: Clear to slightly yellowish oil, soluble in alcohol, ether and glacial acetic acid. Made by steam distilling the flowers of *Rosmarinus officinalis*.

ROSIN: Translucent amber chips, soluble in alcohol, ether, glacial acetic acid and oil. Derived by steam distillation of the sap of pine trees.

ROTTENSTONE (tripoli): White abrasive powder. Crushed and milled from rock.

SALICYLIC ACID (ortho-hydroxy benzoic acid): White powder, soluble in alcohol, oil of turpentine and ether. Made by treating a hot solution of sodium phenolate with carbon dioxide.

SAND (silicon dioxide): White crystals or powder, soluble only in hydrofluoric acid or molten alkali. Found widely in its natural state. Can also be made from a soluble silicate (waterglass) by acidifying, washing and igniting.

SESAME OIL (benne oil, teel oil): Bland yellow liquid, soluble in chloroform, ether and carbon disulfide. Extracted from the plant *Sesamum indicum*, found in China, Japan, and South America.

SHELLAC (garmet lac; gum lac; stick lac): A natural resin secreted by the insect Laccifer and deposited on the trees in India. Soluble in alcohol.

SILICA GEL: Hard white lumps, crystals or powder. Regenerative adsorbent, having a vast internal porosity in relation to its outside surface. Made by the reaction of sulfuric acid and sodium silicate.

SILICONE WATER EMULSION: A milky slippery liquid that can be further diluted with water to any desired concentration. Made by the mixture of silicone oil, emulsifier and water.

SILVER NITRATE: Transparent crystals, soluble in cold water or hot alcohol. Made by dissolving silver in dilute nitric acid and evaporating. Caution: Highly toxic. Strong irritant, handle with care.

SODA ASH (sodium carbonate): Grayish white powder, soluble in water. Mined in areas such as Great Salt Lake, or can be made by the Solvay ammonia soda process.

SODIUM ALGINATE: Colorless to light yellow solid, may be in granular or powdered form. Forms a thick collodial solution with water. Made by extraction from brown seaweed (kelp).

SODIUM ALUMINATE: White powder, soluble in water. Made by heating bauxite with sodium carbonate and extracting the sodium aluminate with water.

SODIUM BICARBONATE (baking soda): White powder, soluble in water. Made by treating a saturated solution of soda ash with carbon dioxide.

SODIUM BISULFATE (niter cake): Colorless crystals soluble in water. A by-product in the manufacture of hydrochloric and nitric acids. Caution: Toxic when in solution. Irritant to eyes and skin.

SODIUM CARBONATE: See *Soda Ash*.

SODIUM CHLORIDE (salt): White crystals soluble in water and glycerol. Made by the evaporation of salt brine.

SODIUM DODECYLBENZENE SULFATE: White to light yellow flakes or powder. Biodegradable.

SODIUM LAURYL SULFATE: White or light yellow crystals, soluble in water. Acts as a wetting agent.

SODIUM METAPHOSPHATE: White powder, soluble in water.

SODIUM METASILICATE: A crystalline silicate. White granules, soluble in water.

SODIUM PENTACHLOROPHENATE: White to tan powder, soluble in water and acetone. Caution: Toxic by ingestion and inhalation. Irritant to eyes and skin.

SODIUM PERBORATE: White odorless powder or crystals. Decomposes in water to release oxygen. Made by electrolysis of a solution of borax and soda ash.

SODIUM PHOSPHATE: White powder, soluble in water and alcohol. Made by precipitating calcium carbonate from a solution of dicalcium phosphate with soda ash.

SODIUM SESQUICARBONATE: White needle shaped crystals, soluble in water. Made by crystallation from a solution of sodium carbonate and sodium bicarbonate.

SODIUM SILICATE (waterglass): Clear viscous liquid, soluble in water. Made by the fusion of sand and soda ash.

SODIUM SULFATE (salt cake): White crystals or powder, soluble in water. A byproduct of hydrochloric acid production from salt and sulfuric acid.

SODIUM SULFITE: White crystals or powder, soluble in water. Made by reacting sulfur dioxide with soda ash and water.

SODIUM THIOSULFATE: White crystals or powder, soluble in water and oil of turpentine. Made by heating a solution of sodium sulfite with powdered sulfur.

SODIUM TRIPOLYPHOSPHATE: White powder, soluble in water. Made by calcination of sodium orthophosphate mixture from sodium carbonate and phosphoric acid.

SOYBEAN OIL (Chinese bean oil, soy oil): Pale yellow drying oil, soluble in alcohol, ether, chloroform or carbon disulfide. Made by expression and solvent extraction of crushed soybeans.

STEARAMIDE: Colorless flakes, soluble in alcohol.

STEARIC ACID: Waxlike solid, soluble in alcohol, ether, chloroform or carbon disulfide. Made hydrogenation of oleic acid.

STODDARD SOLVENT: Water-white liquid solvent. Mildly flammable.

SULFITE LIQUOR: A waste liquor from the sulfite paper making process. Synthetic vanilla (vanalin) is made from this material.

SULFONATED CASTOR OIL: A vegetable oil that has been treated with sulfuric acid and neutralized with a small amount of caustic soda. The oil is then emulsifyable with water.

SUPERPHOSPHATE (acid phosphate): Water-soluble powder, made by the action of sulfuric acid on insoluble rock.

TALC (talcum, mineral graphite, steatite): A mined mineral (magnesium silicate) white gray pearly color with a greasy feel.

TANNIC ACID (gallotainic acid, tannin): Light yellow crystals, soluble in water, alcohol and benzene. Made by extraction of nutgalls and tree bark, with water and alcohol. Caution: Moderately toxic by ingestion and inhalation.

TARTARIC ACID: White crystalline powder, soluble in water and alcohol. Made from maleic anhydride and hydrogen peroxide.

TIN, POWDERED (stannum): White ductile solid. Metallic element of atomic number 50, group IVA of the periodic system.

TINCTURE OF BENZOIN: Clear to pale yellow liquid having a slight camphor odor. The crystals from which the tincture is made, are derived from the condensation of benzaldehyde in a cyanide solution.

TINCTURE OF RHUBARB: Dried root and stalks of rhubarb are treated with alcohol to form a tincture (about 10% solution).

TITANIUM DIOXIDE (titanium white, titania): White powder, miscible with water, alcohol or oil. Made by treating ilmenite with sulfuric acid.

TRAGACANTH (tragacanth gum): White flakes or yellow powder. Soluble in alkaline solution.

TRICHLOROETHYLENE (tri, trichlor): Colorless heavy liquid, slightly soluble in water, miscible with organic solvents. Made from tetrachloroethane by treatment with alkali in the presence of water. Caution: Vapors toxic. Use with adequate ventilation.

TRISODIUM PHOSPHATE (sodium phosphate dibasic): Colorless crystals or white powder, soluble in water and alcohol. Made by precipitating calcium carbonate from a solution of dicalcium phosphate with soda ash.

TURPENTINE: Colorless clear oily liquid. Made by steam distillation of turpentine gum. Caution: Toxic if taken internally. Flammable. Handle with care.

ULTRAMARINE BLUE: Blue lumps, soluble in oil. Made by heating a mixture of sulfur, clay, alkali and reducer at high temperatures.

VERMICULITE: Crystalline type structure with high porosity. Insoluble, except in hot acids. Used as a filler in concrete, and for thermal insulation.

VINEGAR (dilute acetic acid): Brown liquid dilutable with water. Made by fermentation of fruit and grains. May be distilled to remove brown color, after which it is known as white vinegar.

WHITE BEESWAX: Wax from the honeycomb of frames in the beehive. White color is obtained by bleaching the natural yellow wax. Soluble in chloroform, ether and oils. Melting point 62°-65°C.

WITCH HAZEL: A clear white astringent liquid, soluble in water and alcohol.

WOOD TAR (pine tar): Viscous sticky brown to black syrup, soluble in alcohol and acetone. Made by the destructive distillation of pine wood.

YELLOW BEESWAX: See white beeswax. Note: Both yellow and white beeswax have the same properties except for color. Therefore, where color is not important such as in floor wax for example, the yellow wax is more economical.

ZINC BROMIDE: White crystalline powder, soluble in water, alcohol and ether. Made by the interaction of solutions of barium bromide and zinc sulphate, and then crystallized.

ZINC CHLORIDE: White crystals or crystalline powder, soluble in water, alcohol and glycerin. Made by the action of hydro-chloric acid on zinc.

ZINC OXIDE (Chinese white, zinc white): Coarse white to gray powder, soluble in acids and alkalies. Made by oxidation of vaporized pure zinc.

ZINC SULFATE (white vitriol): Colorless crystalline powder, soluble in water or glyceral. Made by the action of sulfuric acid on zinc oxide.

APPENDIX G

A Treatise on Denatured Alcohols

$$\begin{array}{ccc} H & & H \\ | & & | \\ H-C & \!\!\!-\!\!\! & C-H \\ | & & | \\ H & & H \end{array}$$

ETHYL ALCOHOL/DENATURED ETHYL ALCOHOL

Alcohols are widely used in many areas of chemistry, and especially in compounding of formulas such as those found in *The Formula Book*. As a matter of fact, it would be hard to conceive of being able to make many of the compounds without it. But, based on the mail we have received from many teachers and students, there seems to be some confusion over the two primary types, i.e., ethyl alcohol in its pure form, and ethyl alcohol that has been denatured, denatured alcohol. We hope this section will promote a better understanding for those who may not be completely clear on the subject.

Ethyl alcohol (ethanol, grain alcohol) (C_2H_5OH or CH_3CH_2OH), is a clear colorless liquid having a melting point of $-117°C.$, and a boiling point of $78.5°C$. It is miscible in any proportion with water or ether, and is soluble in a sodium hydroxide (caustic soda) solution. Flammable, it burns in air with a bluish transparent flame, producing water and carbon dioxide as it burns. Density is 0.789 at 20°C.

Absolute (anhydrous) ethyl alcohol is obtained by the removal of water. One process for accomplishing this is to react the water in the alcohol, with calcium oxide and then distill the alcohol.

Ethyl alcohol is made by (A) the fermentation of grains and fruits, and also directly from dextrose, (B) by absorption of ethylene from coal or petroleum gas, and then water reaction,

184

and (C) by the reduction of acetaldehyde in the presence of a catalyst.

Ethyl alcohol is used in tremendous quantities in beverages which are taxed by the federal government. There are many other uses as well, such as in pharmaceuticals, tinctures, and extracts for internal use, where it is not taxed as it is for beverages. For these uses however, a special tax-free permit must be obtained from the Alcohol and Tobacco Unit of the Federal government. Permits of this type are available to educational institutions as well. However, for small quantity use, just buying a bottle of 95 or 100 proof vodka is much less complicated.

Denatured alcohol is ethyl alcohol (the same as is used in beverages), except that it has been adulterated with other chemicals that make it unfit for beverage use, while still retaining its other characteristics. Therefore, denatured alcohol is not taxed as pure ethyl alcohol is, making it very much less expensive.

There are two basic types of denatured alcohol, Completely Denatured (CDA), and Specially Denatured (SDA). The denaturants that are used are specified by the Alcohol and Tobacco Tax Unit, and depend on the end use of the alcohol. For example, a denaturant acceptable for use in alcohol to be used as an industrial solvent would be entirely unacceptable for use in a body lotion or mouthwash because of its degree of toxicity and irritating properties. Therefore, the type of denatured alcohol must be chosen for the compound it's to be used in. Following is a list of general compound classifications and the code number of the denatured alcohol approved for each. You will notice that a given type of denaturant may be used in the alcohol that is used in many different formulas. From the following chart it will be seen that Specially Denatured Alcohol, Type 40, is approved for use in a number of applications such as: bath preparations, bay rum, cleaning solutions, colognes, etc. Therefore, in purchasing denatured alcohol it is practical to select the type that fits as many uses as possible. While the approved types of denatured alcohol for specific uses is mandatory for a manufacturer who resells, it does not apply to the individual making the product for his own use. However, in the interest of safety, it is *highly recommended* that only approved types for the specific formulas be used.

185

Appendix G

DENATURED ALCOHOL USE	ALCOHOL and TOBACCO TAX APPROVED TYPE
Animal Feed Supplements	35A.
Antifreeze	1.
Antiseptic Bathing Solutions	46.
Antiseptic Solutions	23A, 37, 38B, 38F.
Bath Preparations	1, 3A, 3B, 23A, 30, 36, 38B, 39B, 39C, 40, 40A, 40B, 40C.
Bay Rum	23A, 37, 38B, 39, 39B, 39D, 40, 40A, 40B, 40C.
Brake Fluids	1, 3A.
Candy Glazes	13A, 23A, 35, 35A.
Cellulose Coatings	1, 23A, 30.
Cleaning Solutions	1, 3A, 23A, 23H, 30, 36, 39B, 40, 40A, 40B, 40C.
Coatings	1, 23A.
Colognes	38B, 39, 39A, 39B, 39C, 40, 40A, 40B, 40C.
Cutting Oils	1, 3A.
Dentifrices	31A, 37, 38B, 38C, 38D.
Deodorants (Body)	23A, 38B, 39B, 39C, 40, 40A, 40B, 40C.

186

Detergents (Home Use)   1, 3A, 23A, 23H, 30, 36, 39B,
                                 40, 40A, 40B, 40C.

Detergents (Industrial)   1, 3A, 23A, 30.

Disinfectants   1, 3A, 3B, 23A, 23H, 27A,
                                 27B, 30, 37, 38B, 39B, 40,
                                 40A, 40B, 40C.

Drugs and Medicinal   1, 2B, 2C, 3A, 6B, 12A, 13A,
   Chemicals   17, 29, 30, 32.

Duplicating Fluids   1, 3A, 30.

Dye Solutions   1, 3A, 23A, 30, 39C, 40, 40A,
                                 40B, 40C.

Fuel Uses   1, 3A, 28A.

Fungicides   1, 3A, 3B, 23A, 23H, 27A,
                                 27B, 30, 37, 38B, 39B, 40,
                                 40A, 40B, 40C.

Hair and Scalp Preparations   3B, 23A, 23F, 23H, 37, 38B,
                                 39, 39A, 39B, 39C, 39D, 40,
                                 40A, 40B, 40C.

Inks   1, 3A, 13A, 23A, 30, 32, 33

Insecticides   1, 3A, 3B, 23A, 23H, 27A,
                                 27B, 30, 37, 38B, 39B, 40,
                                 40A, 40B, 40C.

Iodine Solutions and   25, 25A.
   Tinctures

Lacquer Thinners   1, 23A.

Liniments	27, 27B, 38B.
Lotions and Creams (Body, Face and Hands)	23A, 23H, 31A, 37, 38B, 39, 39B, 39C, 40, 40A, 40B, 40C.
Mouthwashes	37, 38B, 38C, 38D, 38F.
Perfumes and Tinctures	38B, 39, 39B, 39C, 40, 40A, 40B, 40C.
Petroleum Products	1, 2B, 3A.
Plastics-Cellulose	1, 2B, 3A, 12A, 13A, 30.
Plastics and Resins	1, 2B, 3A, 12A, 13A, 30.
Polishes	1, 3A, 30, 40, 40A, 40B, 40C.
Preserving Solutions	1, 3A, 12A, 13A, 22, 23A, 30, 32, 37, 38B, 42, 44.
Resin Coating (Natural)	1, 23A.
Resin Coating (Synthetic)	1, 23A, 30.
Room Deodorants	3A, 22, 37, 38B, 39B, 39C, 40, 40A, 40B, 40C.
Rubbing Alcohol	23H.
Scientific Instruments	1, 3A.
Shampoos	1, 3A, 3B, 23A, 27B, 31A, 36, 38B, 39A, 39B, 40, 40A, 40B, 40C.

Shellac Coatings	1, 23A.
Soaps (Industrial)	1, 3A, 23A, 30.
Soaps (Toilet)	1, 3A, 3B, 23A, 30, 3C, 38B, 39B, 39C, 40, 40A, 40B, 40C.
Soldering Flux	1, 3A, 23A, 30.
Solutions (Miscellaneous)	1, 3A, 23A, 30, 39B, 40, 40A, 40B, 40C.
Solvents and Thinners	1, 23A.
Stains (Wood)	1, 3A, 23A, 30.
Sterilizing Solutions	1, 3A, 12A, 13A, 22, 23A, 30, 32, 37, 38B, 42, 44.
Toilet Water	38B, 39, 39A, 39B, 39C, 40, 40A, 40B, 40C.
Unclassified Uses	1, 3A.
Vinegar	18, 29, 35A.

DENATURING FORMULAS

While the formulas for denaturing ethyl alcohol for various applications are not particularly relevant to the user of *The Formula Book* because the alcohol you purchase will already be denatured, they are of general interest in that they show the different degrees of contamination required for uses in different product formulas. For this reason they are included in this section.

189

Appendix G

ALCOHOL & TOBACCO TAX,
APPROVED TYPES   DENATURING FORMULAS

1)   100 gallons ethyl alcohol, 5 gallons wood alcohol.

2B)   100 gallons ethyl alcohol, 5 gallons methyl alcohol.

2C)   100 gallons ethyl alcohol, 33 pounds metallic sodium and 1/2 gallon benzene.

3A)   100 gallons ethyl alcohol, 5 gallons methyl alcohol.

3B)   100 gallons ethyl alcohol, 1 gallon pine tar.

6B)   100 gallons ethyl alcohol, 1/2 gallon pyridine bases.

12A) 100 gallons ethyl alcohol, 5 gallons benzene.

13A) 100 gallons ethyl alcohol, 10 gallons ethyl ether.

17)   100 gallons ethyl alcohol, 6.4 fl. oz. bone oil.

18)   100 gallons ethyl alcohol, 100 gallons vinegar (90Gr.)

23A) 100 gallons ethyl alcohol, 10 gallons acetone.

23F) 100 gallons ethyl alcohol, 3 pounds salicylic acid, USP, 1 pound resorcin, USP, 1 gallon bay oil, USP.

23H) 100 gallons ethyl alcohol, 8 gallons acetone, 1.5 gallons methyl isobutyl ketone.

27A) 100 gallons ethyl alcohol, 35 pounds camphor, USP, 1 gallon clove oil, USP.

27B) 100 gallons ethyl alcohol, 1 gallon lavender oil, USP, 100 pounds medicinal soft soap, USP.

28A) 100 gallons ethyl alcohol, 1 gallon gasoline.

190

29) 100 gallons ethyl alcohol, 1 gallon 100% acetaldehyde.

30) 100 gallons ethyl alcohol, 10 gallons methyl alcohol.

31A) 100 gallons ethyl alcohol, 100 pounds glycerol, USP, 20 pounds hard soap.

32) 100 gallons ethyl alcohol, 5 gallons ethyl ether.

37) 100 gallons ethyl alcohol, 45 fluid ounces eucalyptol USP, 30 ounces by weight thymol, 20 ounces by weight menthol USP.

38B) 100 gallons ethyl alcohol, 10 pounds menthol, USP.

38C) 100 gallons ethyl alcohol, 10 pounds menthol, USP, 1.25 gallons formaldehyde, USP.

38F) 100 gallons ethyl alcohol, 6 pounds boric acid, USP, 1-1/3 pounds thymol, 1-1/3 pounds chlorothymol, and 1-1/3 pounds menthol, USP.

39) 100 gallons ethyl alcohol, 9 pounds sodium salicylate USP, 1.25 gallons extract of quassia, 1/8 gallon tert.-butyl alcohol.

39A) 100 gallons ethyl alcohol, 60 ounces quinine, 1/8 gallon tert.-butyl alcohol.

39B) 100 gallons ethyl alcohol, 2-1/2 gallons diethyl phthalate, 1/8 gallon tert.-butyl alcohol.

39C) 100 gallons ethyl alcohol, 1 gallon diethyl phthalate.

39D) 100 gallons ethyl alcohol, 1 gallon bay oil, 50 ounces by weight quinine sulphate.

40)   100 gallons ethyl alcohol, 1-1/2 ounces brucine, 1/8 gallon tert.-butyl alcohol.

40A)   100 gallons ethyl alcohol, 1 pound sucrose octaacetate, 1/8 gallon tert.-butyl alcohol.

40B)   100 gallons ethyl alcohol, 1/16 ounce denatonium benzonate, 1/8 gallon tert.-butyl alcohol.

40C)   100 gallons ethyl alcohol, 3 gallons tert.-butyl alcohol.

42)   100 gallons ethyl alcohol, 80 grams potassium iodine, USP, 109 grams red mecuric iodide.

44)   100 gallons ethyl alcohol, 10 gallons n-butyl alcohol.

APPENDIX H

Selection of Materials

$$H-\underset{\underset{H}{|}}{\overset{\overset{H}{|}}{C}}----\underset{\underset{H}{|}}{\overset{\overset{H}{|}}{C}}-H$$

The selection of materials depends on the end use of the product. For example, the selection of denatured alcohol for use in a paint or varnish thinner would be entirely different from the choice of a product that would be in contact with the skin. (See Appendix F).

There are two basic grades of chemicals used: 1) U.S.P., and 2) Manufacturing or Technical.

1. *U.S.P.*, is an abbreviation for the United States Pharmocopea which is the official federal book of chemicals and drugs. This publication sets up the standards of purity and other specifications that the manufacturer must comply with. Generally speaking, U.S.P. grades are used in compounds that are taken internally, or come in contact with delicate areas of the body that require pure materials. An example of this is where a material such as magnesium sulfate (epsom salts) is contained in a product for internal use, it must be U.S.P. grade.

2. *Manufacturing or Technical Grade.*
In this category, the standards for purity are understandably less than in the U.S.P. grade, in that the end product does not directly affect human health. For example, if the epsom salts were to be used in a foot bath, the purity requirements would not be the same as for internal use, and the Manufacturing or Technical grade would be acceptable.

There is a substantial difference in the cost of these two

grades of materials, therefore, the selection should always be made on the basis of the end use.

The *odor and color*, used in a preparation is largely a matter of personal choice, and usually has no effect on the function of the compound itself. For example, in the formula for After-Shave Lotion, the perfume in the product has no effect on the properties it imparts to the skin. However, if perfume or color is desired, it must be of a type that is compatible with the compound it is to be used in.

Dyes and perfumes fall into three general categories: (1) those that are soluble in oil, (2) those that are soluble in water or alcohol, and (3) those that are suitable for use in an emulsion.

Examples of these types are as follows:

Type One; is soluble in oil and would be used in liquids, semisolids, and solids having an oil base such as Baby Oil.

Type Two; is soluble in water and alcohol and would therefore be used in compounds such as After-Shave Lotion where the base is water and alcohol.

Type Three; is an emulsion type and logically, is used in emulsions. Each formula that requires a perfume or dye has the type specified in the formula itself.

But a word of warning. Perfumes and dyes are in highly concentrated form, and should be used very sparingly.

APPENDIX I

Utensils and Equipment

$$H-\overset{\displaystyle H}{\underset{\displaystyle H}{C}}-\overset{\displaystyle H}{\underset{\displaystyle H}{C}}-H$$

The formulas found in *The Formula Book* are designed for small volumes of the finished product, requiring a minimum of equipment to formulate. The following utensils are required.

1. Several glass measuring cups. (See Figure 2 Appendix J).

2. A set of mixing bowls made of glass, ceramic or plastic. (See Figure 10 Appendix J).

3. A wood fork with spacing of about 1/8" between tines. (See Figure 3, Appendix J).

4. An egg beater. (See Figure 4, Appendix J). An electric mixer, with beaters and bowl, is helpful but not essential. If it has variable speeds, it can be used for both wet and dry mixing, saving a great deal of time and assuring a "good blend."

5. A stem type thermometer is convenient, but again, not absolutely essential. (See Figure 5, Appendix J). If one is not available, remember that water gives off a mild vapor at 140°F., a moderate vapor at 160°F., a heavy vapor at 180°F. and heavy steam at the boiling point.

6. A supply of wood tongue depressors. (See Figure 8, Appendix J). These are smooth, cheap and readily available from any druggist. They make excellent mixing sticks, and are inexpensive enough to be disposable, eliminating a lot of "cleaning up."

7. Paper cups are ideal for small batch formulating. They are inexpensive, disposable and can be easily numbered or marked with a felt marker. (See Figure 1, Appendix J).

195

8. Double boilers are required in many instances. These should be Pyrex. (See Figure 6, Appendix J).

9. A rubber syringe for measuring out drops. (See Figure 7, Appendix J).

10. A set of standard measuring spoons. (See Figure 11a, Appendix J).

11. A plastic cone and filter paper, such as is used in coffee making. (See Figure 9, Appendix J). While filtering a liquid compound after it is finished is not usually essential, it is always desirable, in that a clearer, better looking product results.

12. Containers for the finished product are a matter of personal preference. In most homes, jars and bottles are available. If they are to be purchased, many supermarkets carry them, and drugstores have them for their own use. Larger quantities can be had from bottle distributors, listed in the Yellow Pages.

All chemicals that are stored in containers should be labeled, regardless of whether they are a raw material or a finished compound. This is basic, and must be followed in the interest of safety. Keep all chemicals out of the reach of children, and note the contents on the label. In this way if a child, or even an unsuspecting adult, should accidentally consume the contents, the doctor would know what treatment to initiate. While these formulas have been chosen with an eye to safety, many materials normally regarded as safe, can be dangerous if taken internally, or to excess. Here's an example of a safe label.

This Bottle Contains _____
Its Ingredient(s) are:

Keep out of reach of children.

Made by _____

Date _____
KEEP BOTTLE SEALED

APPENDIX J

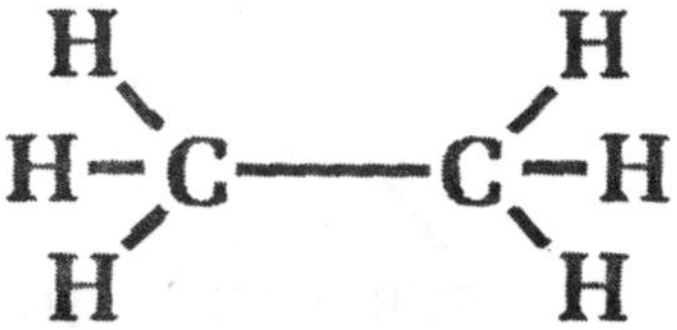

$$H-C-C-H$$

with H atoms above and below each C:

H   H
H—C———C—H
H   H

ILLUSTRATIONS

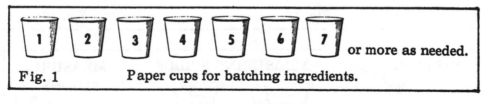

| 1 | 2 | 3 | 4 | 5 | 6 | 7 | or more as needed.

Fig. 1   Paper cups for batching ingredients.

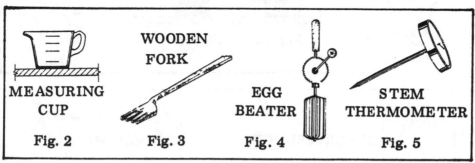

MEASURING CUP
Fig. 2

WOODEN FORK
Fig. 3

EGG BEATER
Fig. 4

STEM THERMOMETER
Fig. 5

197

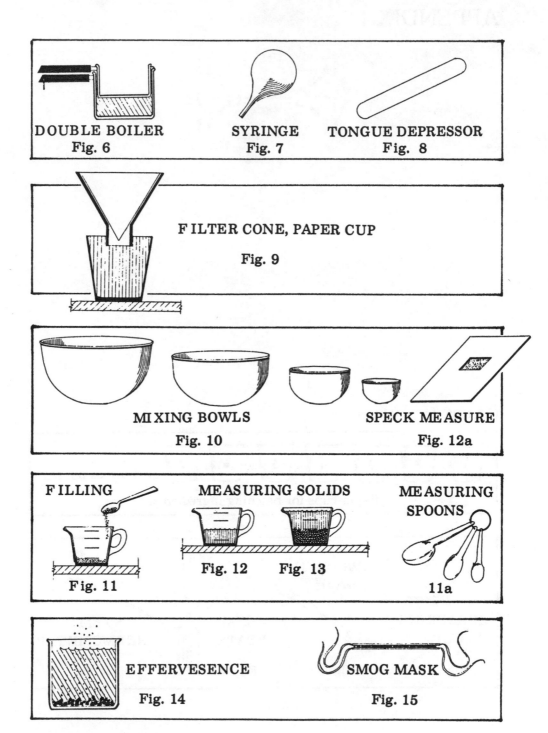

DOUBLE BOILER
Fig. 6

SYRINGE
Fig. 7

TONGUE DEPRESSOR
Fig. 8

FILTER CONE, PAPER CUP

Fig. 9

MIXING BOWLS
Fig. 10

SPECK MEASURE
Fig. 12a

FILLING
Fig. 11

MEASURING SOLIDS
Fig. 12   Fig. 13

MEASURING SPOONS
11a

EFFERVESENCE
Fig. 14

SMOG MASK
Fig. 15

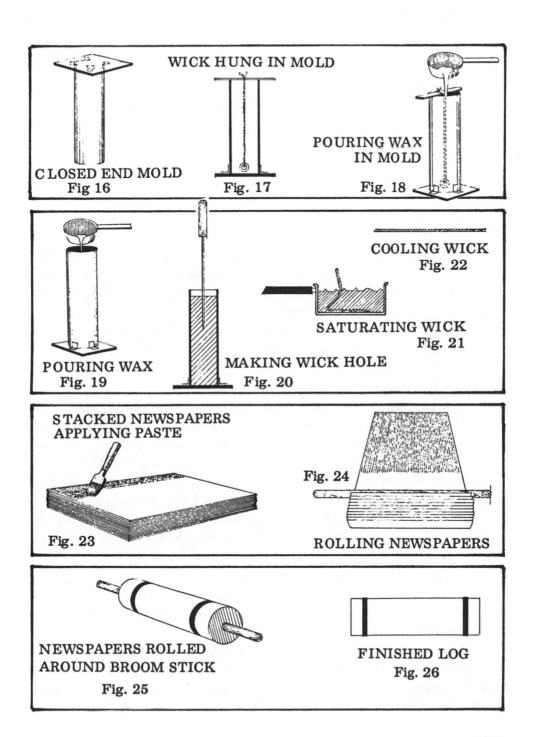

WICK HUNG IN MOLD

CLOSED END MOLD
Fig 16

Fig. 17

POURING WAX
IN MOLD
Fig. 18

POURING WAX
Fig. 19

MAKING WICK HOLE
Fig. 20

SATURATING WICK
Fig. 21

COOLING WICK
Fig. 22

STACKED NEWSPAPERS
APPLYING PASTE

Fig. 23

Fig. 24

ROLLING NEWSPAPERS

NEWSPAPERS ROLLED
AROUND BROOM STICK
Fig. 25

FINISHED LOG
Fig. 26

APPENDIX K

Formulating Procedures

$$H-\underset{\underset{H}{|}}{\overset{\overset{H}{|}}{C}}---\underset{\underset{H}{|}}{\overset{\overset{H}{|}}{C}}-H$$

The ingredients in each formula must be combined in the correct sequence, because a chemical reaction may take place and a deviation from that sequence could prevent it. One of the best ways to insure against error is to use separate containers for the ingredients, numbered in the order that they are to be incorporated into the compound. (See Appendix J, Figure 1.) Paper cups work well for this, in that they are inexpensive, disposable, and can be easily numbered with a felt marker.

The correct measurement of ingredients is important. Always have the utensil that is being measured into on a level surface. (See Figure 2, Appendix J.) Measure accurately to the line of the quantity specified. Avoid touching container to eliminate the possibility of compacting the material, which would increase its quantity. (See Figure 11, Appendix J.)

Use standard measuring spoons. Not eating spoons. A spoonful is a measuring spoon that is filled level with the top. Dip spoon in material to rounding, and then scrape excess off with a knife. (Figure 11a, Appendix J.)

A speck is the amount of powdered or granular material that will lie in a 1/4" square marked on a piece of paper. (See Figure 12a, Appendix J.)

When a formula calls for a portion of a cup of lump or semisolid material that is not *water soluble*, use this method. If you want to measure 1/2 cup of lump paraffin for example, pour *cold* water in a measuring cup to the 1/2 cup line. Next, add

200

lumps of paraffin to the water until the water level reaches the 1 cup line. Pour out the water, and the paraffin in the cup will equal 1/2 cup. (See Figures 12 and 13, Appendix J.)

Follow instructions given in each individual formula, and *always* follow labeling instructions given in Appendix I.

MEMOS

This Bottle Contains _____
Its Ingredient(s) are:

Keep out of reach of children.

Made by _____

Date _____
            KEEP BOTTLE SEALED

This Bottle Contains _____
Its Ingredient(s) are:

Keep out of reach of children.

Made by _____

Date _____
            KEEP BOTTLE SEALED

This Bottle Contains _____
Its Ingredient(s) are:

Keep out of reach of children.

Made by _____

Date _____
            KEEP BOTTLE SEALED

This Bottle Contains _____
Its Ingredient(s) are:

Keep out of reach of children.

Made by _____

Date _____
            KEEP BOTTLE SEALED

This Bottle Contains _____
Its Ingredient(s) are:

Keep out of reach of children.

Made by _____

Date _____
            KEEP BOTTLE SEALED

This Bottle Contains _____
Its Ingredient(s) are:

Keep out of reach of children.

Made by _____

Date _____
            KEEP BOTTLE SEALED

This Bottle Contains _____
Its Ingredient(s) are:

Keep out of reach of children.

Made by _____

Date _____
            KEEP BOTTLE SEALED

This Bottle Contains _____
Its Ingredient(s) are:

Keep out of reach of children.

Made by _____

Date _____
            KEEP BOTTLE SEALED

This Bottle Contains _____
Its Ingredient(s) are:

Keep out of reach of children.

Made by _____

Date _____
            KEEP BOTTLE SEALED

This Bottle Contains _____
Its Ingredient(s) are:

Keep out of reach of children.

Made by _____

Date _____
            KEEP BOTTLE SEALED

This Bottle Contains _____
Its Ingredient(s) are:

Keep out of reach of children.

Made by _____

Date _____
            KEEP BOTTLE SEALED

This Bottle Contains _____
Its Ingredient(s) are:

Keep out of reach of children.

Made by _____

Date _____
            KEEP BOTTLE SEALED

Index

Acne lotion, 77
Additive for heavily soiled
    laundry, 31
After-shave lotion, 76
Alcohol resistant finish for wood,
    26
    rubbing, 70
    solid fuel, 44
Algae spray for ponds, 98
Almonds, lemons, and limes
    cream, 69
Allover skin cream, 75
All purpose germicidal cream, 69
Aluminum cleaner, 39
    polish, 39
Ammonia cleaning powder, 36
Ammonia, household, 36
    household substitute, 36
An American mouthwash, 80
Antacid liquid, 56
Ant exterminator, 48
    mound eradicator, 98
Antifog preparation, 86
Antifreeze, 88
Antiperspirant liquid, 70
Antirust tool coating, 91
Astringent lotion, 70
Athlete's foot powder, 82

Baby oil, 71

Basic soap, 62
Battery terminal protective
    coating, 89
Beauty mask, 74
Bedbug exterminator, 49
Bleach, laundry, 31
Blond hair rinse, 64
Bluing, gun, 104
    laundry, 32
Body and face powder, 76
Book cover coating, 59
Bottle and jar cleaner, 29
Brass polish, 39
Bubble bath, 72
Burn treatment, 72

Candles, 57
Canvas, waterproofing, 28
Car, antifog preparation, 86
    liquid wax, 84
    paste wax, 84
    soap, 84
Carpenter ant exterminator, 99
Carpet cleaner, 23
Cereals and flour, storing, 55
Chapped hands, lotion for, 73
    lips, cream for, 73
Charcoal lighter, 44
Chimney soot remover, 47
Clay, modeling, 58

Index

Cleaner, aluminum, 39
  bottle and jar, 29
  carpet, 23
  concrete, 22
  drain, 37
  garage floor, 91
  glass spray, 37
  golf ball, 105
  golf club, 106
  gun barrel, 105
  hairbrush and comb, 66
  hand, 38
  lens, 40
  marble, 23
  metal, 38
  oven, 54
  paint brush, 51
  porcelain, 40
  radiator, 86
  tile and household, 22
  toilet bowl, 41
  type, 61
  upholstery, 41
  wall and woodwork, 37
  wig and hairpiece, 66
  windshield, 85
Cockroach exterminator, 48
Cold cream, 75
Cologne, 69
Comb and hairbrush cleaner, 66
Composting, 95
Concrete cleaner, 22
  dustproofer, 22
  waterproofing, 21
Contact lens fluid, 81
Cooling hand lotion, 73
Cosmetic remover, 77
Cream, almonds, lemons, and
    limes, 69
  chapped lip, 73
  cold, 75
  deodorant, 71
  germicidal, 69
  glycerin skin gel, 69
  skin, 75
Cucumber skin lotion, 68

Dandelion plant and root killer, 97
Denture adhesive, 79
Denture cleaner, foaming, 79
  nonfoaming, 79
Deodorant cream, 71
  powder, 71
Deodorizer, refrigerator, 54
Detergent, dishwasher, 29
  laundry, 31
  liquid for dishwashing, 29
Dishwasher detergent, 29
Disinfectant, 36
Drain cleaner, 37
  opener, 37
  root destroyer for, 60
Dustproofing, concrete, 22

Easy solid fuel, 103
Electric after-shave lotion, 76
  pre-shave lotion, 77
Engine and parts degreasing
    compound, 90
Exterminator, ant, 48
  bedbug, 49
  carpenter ant, 99
  cockroach, 48
  fly, 48
Extracts of special flavors, 53
Eyewash, soothing, 80

Fabric softener, 33
Face wash, 75
Fence post preservative, 94
Fertilizer for azaleas, 93
  house plants, 93
Fingernail hardener, 74
  softener, 74
Fire extinguisher, 46
Fireplace starter, 44
Fireproofing Christmas trees, 47
  cloth, 46
  wood, 27
Firewood substitute, 45
Flea soap, 100
Floor mop oil, 21
  sweeping compound, 20

Floors, wood, bleach for, 18
  cleaner, 18
  liquid wax, 18
  nonslip wax, 19
  paste wax, 20
Flours and cereals, storing, 55
Flowers, preserving cut, 58
Fly spray, 48
Foaming denture cleaner, 79
Foot bath, soothing, 81
Fuel, alcohol solid, 44
  easy solid, 103
  improver for oil furnaces, 60
Furnaces, fuel improver for oil, 60
Furniture finishing polish, 25
  lemon oil polish, 25
  removing water spots from, 27
  silicone polish, 26
  thin film polish, 26
  water emulsion polish, 26
  wax polish, 25

Galvanized coating repair, 59
Garage floor cleaner, 91
Garden insecticide, 99
Gasoline antiknock additive, 89
  engine cleaning additive, 89
Glass scratch remover, 38
  spray cleaner, 37
Glue, library, 59
Glycerin skin gel, 69
Gold polish, 40
Golf ball cleaner, 105
  club cleaner, 106
  club grip wax, 106
  tees, 106
Grass killer, 97
Grease spot remover, 41
Growing and drying herbs, 55
Gun barrel cleaning solvent, 105
  bluing, 104
  cleaning oil, 104
  lubricant, 105

Hair conditioning cream, 65
  rinse, blond, 64

rinse, lemon 65
set spray, 65
tonic, 66
wave lotion, 66
Hairbrush and comb cleaner, 66
Hairpiece and wig cleaner, 66
Hand cleaner for grease and grime, 38
  lotion, 73
Heavy-duty hand soap, 63
Herbs, growing and drying, 55
Honey and almond lotion, 68
Horse hoof grease, 101
Household ammonia, 36
  ammonia substitute, 36
House plants, fertilizer for, 93

Ink spot remover, 41
Insecticide, garden, 99
Insect repellent, 103
  for animals, 100

Japanese beetle spray for trees and bushes, 99
Jar and bottle sealer, 53

Lamps and torches, oil for, 45
Laundry, additive for heavily soiled, 31
  bleach, 31
  bluing, 32
  detergent, 31
  fabric softener for, 33
  starch, 32
  water softener for, 29
Leak seal for radiators, 86
  tires, 88
Leather preservative, 34
  waterproofing, 35
Lemon hair rinse, 65
Lemon oil furniture polish, 25
Lens cleaner, 40
Library glue, 59
Lighter fluid, 61
Linoleum polish, 20

Index

Liquid detergent for dishwashing, 29
Liquid mascara, 77
Lotion, acne, 77
  after-shave, 76
  astringent, 70
  chapped hands, 73
  cucumber skin, 68
  electric after-shave, 76
  electric pre-shave, 77
  hand, 73
  honey and almond, 68
  suntan, 72
  wrinkle, 74
Lubricating oil, 90
Luminaries, 58

Marble cleaning powder, 23
Mascara, liquid, 77
Mask, beauty, 74
Metal cleaner, 38
  polish, 38
Mildewproofing, 28
Mildewproofing paint, 52
Mineral oil emulsion for tile
    floors, 24
Modeling clay, 58
Moisture protection, 59
Mold stain remover, 33
Mothproofing, 49
Mouse and rat hole sealer, 49
Mouthwash, American, 80
  Swedish, 80
Muscles, rub for stiff, 70

Net preservative, 107
Nonfoaming denture cleaner, 79

Oil for lamps and torches, 45
Oven cleaner, 54

Paint and varnish remover, 51
Paint brush cleaner, 51
  softening old, 50

Paint, mildewproofing, 52
  remover, 51
  spot remover, 52
Perspiration stain remover, 33
Petroleum jelly, 73
Poison, rat, 50
Polish, aluminum, 39
  brass, 39
  furniture finishing, 25
  furniture lemon oil, 25
  furniture silicone, 26
  furniture thin film, 26
  furniture water emulsion, 26
  furniture wax, 25
  gold, 40
  linoleum, 20
  metal, 38
  silver, 39
Polishing cloth, 85
Ponds, algae spray for, 98
Porcelain cleaner, 40
Powder, ammonia cleaning, 36
  athlete's foot, 82
  body and face, 76
  deodorant, 71
  marble cleaning, 23
Preservative, fence post, 94
  leather, 34
  net, 107
Preserving cut flowers, 58

Rabbit repellent, 99
Radiator cleaner, 86
  leak sealer, 86
  rust preventer, 88
  rust remover, 87
  scale preventer, 87
  scale remover, 87
Refreshing face wash, 75
Refrigerator deodorizer, 54
Removing water spots from
    furniture, 27
Repellent, insect, 100, 103
  rabbit, 99

208

Root destroyer for drains, 60
Rubbing alcohol, 70
Rust stain remover, 34

Saddle soap, 35
Salt blocks, 101
Saving soap, 56
Scratch remover, glass, 38
Septic tank reactivator, 60
Shampoo, 64
Silver polish, 39
Skin softener, 76
Ski wax, 104
Snow and ice melting compound, 61
Soap, basic, 62
  car, 84
  flea, 100
  hand, 63, 64
  saddle, 35
  saving, 56
Softener, fabric, 33
  fingernail, 74
  skin, 76
  water, 29
Softening an old paint brush, 50
Solid fuel, alcohol, 44
  easy, 103
Soothing eyewash, 80
  foot bath, 81
Spices, storing, 55
Spot remover, grease, 41
  ink, 41
  paint, 52
  water, 27
Stain remover, mold, 33
  perspiration, 33
  rust, 34
Starch, laundry, 32
Stiff muscle rub, 70
Storing flour and cereals, 55
  spices, 55
Suntan lotion, 72
Swedish formula mouthwash, 80

Termite proofing, 27
Tile and household cleaner, 22
Tile floors, mineral oil emulsion for, 24
Toilet bowl cleaner, 41
Tool rust remover, 91
Toothpaste, 79
Trees and shrubs, Japanese beetle spray for, 99
  wound dressing for, 94
Type cleaner, 61

Upholstery cleaner, 41

Wall and woodwork cleaner, 37
Waterless hand soap, 64
Waterproofing canvas, 28
  concrete, 21
  leather, 35
Water softener for dishes or laundry, 29
Wax, car paste, 84
  furniture polish, 25
  liquid car, 84
  nonslip wood floor, 19
  ski, 104
  wood floor liquid, 18
  wood floor paste, 20
Whipped cream improver, 53
Whitewash, 94
Wig and hairpiece cleaner, 66
Window cleaner spray, 42
Windshield cleaning and de-icing, 85
Wood, alcohol resistant finish for, 26
  fireproofing, 27
Wood floor bleach, 18
  cleaner, 18
  liquid wax, 18
  nonslip wax, 19
  paste wax, 20
Wound dressing for trees and shrubs, 94
Wrinkle lotion for skin, 74

Norman Stark, who holds over a dozen patents on his inventions, has met with remarkable success in his supplementary textbook *The Formula Manual*, from which this book evolved. *The Formula Manual* has been sold to thousands of school libraries and chemistry departments since Stark first began working on it in 1970.

His work in this area has required considerable expansion; he has established his own laboratory in Tucson for analyzing existing products, creating new formulas, and undertaking thorough testing of his formulas.

Stark's work in chemistry goes back to 1940, when he founded the Stark Research Corporation to conduct research, development, and manufacturing in the chemical field.

Shortly after the beginning of World War II, Stark was asked by the military to develop a process for making fuel tablets —small bars of a combination of wax and finely ground wood flour encased in a chemically impregnated carton—to be used to heat field rations. After making millions of fuel tablets, Stark was then put to work developing a high-speed process for making the Sterno-type canned heat. Finally, during the war, Stark was commissioned to develop a continuous high-speed process for making candles, a need created by the fact that troops were moving ahead of generating equipment on the fighting fronts and were in desperate need of light.

After the end of the war, Stark discontinued the manufacturing aspects of his concern and devoted his efforts solely to research and development. Since that time, many of his projects have resulted in patents and licensing agreements with America's leading corporations. Frequently, when Stark licensed a process or a material, he would act as a consultant to the company involved.